Comic Strip Toys

By Kenny Harman

Published by
Wallace-Homestead Book Co.
Des Moines, Iowa 50305

Kenny Harman, a young man interested in old things, is 29 years old. A Nebraskan, he grew up in Lincoln, graduated from Nebraska Wesleyan University, and now teaches first grade in the Lincoln Public Schools. He spent two years traveling in Europe.

Kenny has been collecting antiques since he was ten, specializing in early tin advertising signs, Victorian furniture, lamps, and, of course, toys. He now has about 500 toys in his collection, mostly comic strip and Lehmann toys.

A fan of old comic strips, he says, "One thing I would like to see is some of the old comic strips brought back to the funny pages again."

Copyright ©1975
KENNY HARMAN

Library of Congress
Catalog Card Number
74-84523

ISBN: 0-87069-078-7

Printed in the U.S.A.

TABLE OF CONTENTS

ACKNOWLEDGMENTS

I would like to express my sincere appreciation for photographs, information, and encouragement to Dale Kelley, publisher of the *Antique Toy World;* Robert Lesser; Don Hillman; A. H. Mundis; and Second Childhood, New York City. I'm especially grateful to my mother and my Uncle George, who helped edit this book; Dave Boyle, with whom I traveled many miles; Funderwhite's Antiques in Eagle, Pennsylvania; Murray Harris, for his help in locating old comic strips from his collection of graphic arts; Bob Walker, a fellow comic strip character toy collector and friend; Ward Kimball, who generously contributed pictures of some of his collection; the Perelman Antique Toy Museum in Phildelphia, which graciously allowed me to photograph toys; and, finally, to my photographer uncle, Ralph Harman, who was responsible for photographing my comic strip character toy collection.

Cast-iron Toonerville Trolley

INTRODUCTION

Comic strip character toys have rapidly become some of the most desirable antique toys of today. They represent an era in American history which brings on nostalgic feelings, a time that seems filled with bliss and devoid of today's complex problems. Comic strips are as representative of America as the Fourth of July or the World Series. While most of the old strips are gone today, many of the toys they inspired remain to remind us of a golden era in American history.

The term "comic strip character toy" has a broader meaning than it would seem to indicate. Personalities from radio, movies, comic books, and television are also included. An endless variety of items representative of these characters have been manufactured from 1896 to the 1960s. This book deals only with toys. Giveaway novelties, such as pins, rings, figurines, and the like, are a completely different hobby, as are dolls. Several toys contained in this book, however, do fall into both the doll and toy categories.

The vast majority of the comic strip character toys that were manufactured are contained in this book. To label any not found pictured or listed as rare is erroneous, as it was a physical impossibility to locate and photograph each and every toy. Wooden toys, with Schoenhut being the exception, are purposely touched upon lightly. Tin and cast-iron toys are the most desirable to comic strip character toy collectors. Therefore, this book primarily deals with these.

Today, few comic strips offer the type of uncomplicated humor or fantastic adventure that millions of Americans loved for so many years. There seems to be hope, however. "Orphan Annie" was recently replaced by the original strip from 1936, and over 300 newspapers have begun to run the old strip. "Krazy Kat" has also returned to several newspapers. Perhaps, if we are lucky, other old loved comic strips can return to the funny pages once again!

Ad for Orphan Annie Skipping Rope

Orphan Annie-Skipping Rope
New, Unique and Clever

When mechanism is wound Orphan Annie skips rope. If she falls she gets up herself to an upright position, never stopping her rope jumping, regardless of whether she falls on her back or on her face. This toy is just as full of pep and action as the Orphan Annie you see in the comics. Height about 5 in. Shpg. wt., 1 lb.
49F5776 .... **25c**

Ad for Happy Hooligan Police Patrol

H9140—"Happy Hooligan" Police Patrol; a large, iron toy, 19 in. long; with 2 galloping horses and gong. Representing "Gloomy Gus" as driver, "Happy" as prisoner, and the "Cop" who beats "Happy" when the wheels revolve. Nicely finished in bright colors. Shipping weight, 10½ lb. Each **$1.00**

THE YELLOW KID

On February 16, 1896, a bald-headed, gap-toothed, flap-eared young urchin, who looked faintly Chinese, marked the real beginning of the American comic strip. He appeared in the three-quarter page cartoon called "The Great Dog Show in M'Googan Avenue" in the *New York Sunday World*. His flour sack nightgown was colored a light yellow, which made him stand out like a bull's-eye on a target. The creator, Richard Outcault, used the nightshirt like a billboard and, almost from the beginning, put messages on it. The gutter style impudence of the young lad endeared him to a great number of the World's readers. Perhaps because so many of them were caught up in the same life-style and environment as Outcault's character, he quickly became the focal point, and the strip was renamed "The Yellow Kid."

"The Yellow Kid" was so popular that William Randolph Hearst, of the *New York Journal*, hired Outcault away from Pulitzer's *New York World*. The offers, counteroffers, and lawsuit that followed were so widely publicized that it gave birth to the phrase, "yellow journalism." Publishers all over the country became acutely aware of the dramatic effect that a comic strip could have on circulation.

Yellow Kid Goat Cart

"The Yellow Kid" was marketed in everything from crackers to cigarettes, but only in two toys. The smallest is a 1½" high, cast-iron cap bomb. A cap is inserted in his mouth, which slides up and down. When the head is dropped onto a hard surface, the cap will explode.

The other toy is a 7½" long, cast-iron goat cart in which the Yellow Kid is a passenger. The goat and cart are cast in two pieces and nickle-plated. The wheels are painted red, while the figure is usually painted black and red or all yellow. The figure is removable.

Even though "The Yellow Kid" was extremely popular among most of his readers, he was discontinued after only two years. His rough character, antics, and poor language caused many parents to rebel. However, the effect "The Yellow Kid" had on the future of the American comic strips was devastating.

Yellow Kid cap bomb

"The Yellow Kid" — five months after his inception

THE KATZENJAMMER KIDS

and

THE CAPTAIN AND THE KIDS

Slapstick comedy was first introduced to the comics in 1897. The originator was Rudolph Dirks and his strip was the immortal "Katzenjammer Kids." Unlike the "The Yellow Kid," there was no overtone of slum life nor of the too well behaved and snobbish character reflected by "Buster Brown." "The Katzenjammer Kids" was hilariously funny, while still seeming to be linked to reality.

The Katzenjammers were a German family consisting of two devilish children named Hans and Fritz, Mamma, der Captain, and an old gentleman called der Inspector. Through wars, depressions, and numerous changes in the American mood, Hans and Fritz have continued to entertain millions with their humorous assaults on law, order, and logic. Their motto is "society iss nix."

In a classic law suit in 1912, Dirks left Hearst's *New York Journal,* but he had to leave the title to his strip and the characters. However, he was granted the right to use his characters under a different title. The result was the continuance of "The Katzenjammer Kids," only now by a new artist, H. Knerr. Dirks went to work for another paper and carried on his strip under a new title, "The Captain and the Kids."

The most widely known of the Katzenjammer toys is often referred to as the spanking toy. It is a 12" long, cast-iron donkey cart that sold for $.45 at the turn of the century. Mamma is animated as she spanks Fritz with each turn of the wheels. There are two minor variations of the toy. One has Hans standing on the rear of the cart, while he is missing from the other. Both toys are painted orange with red wheels, while the figures are in lifelike colors.

Shortly after the turn of the century, the Kenton Hardware Company, of Kenton, Ohio, introduced the Mamma Katzenjammer Bank. The action of this mechanical, cast-iron bank allows Mamma's eyes to roll when a coin is inserted in a slot in her back.

A lady who resembled Mamma Katzenjammer was produced in a small, silver and green, kicking donkey cart. Mamma is a removable figure. Whether this was originally sold as Mamma Katzenjammer is pure speculation.

Around 1911, Kenton produced a 10½" long, cast-iron "Sight Seeing Auto." There was also a minor name variation, "Seeing New York." In the very early days of the strips, a few artists got together on several occasions and each drew his character or characters into one special Sunday strip. Similarly, characters from two artists were employed as the occupants of the bus. They were Uncle Heine and Mamma from Dirk's "Katzenjammer Kids," Gloomy Gus and Happy Hooligan from Opper's "Happy Hooligan," and a fat Frenchman from Opper's "Alphonse and Gaston." Unfortunately, all the figures are removable and are almost never found today with the bus. However, the figures have been reproduced and are available to anyone who is fortunate enough to find a bus. While reproduced figures add almost nothing to the antique value of a toy, they do greatly enhance the original appearance of the toy.

Mamma Katzenjammer in a Cart

H9132—"Katzenjammer" Donkey Cart, representing Uncle Heine as driver, Mamma with Fritz on her knee being spanked when the wheels revolve, and Hans standing at the end of the cart crying. All nicely finished in bright colors. Full length, 12 in. Shipping weight, 4 lb. Each.....45c.

Ad for Katzenjammer Donkey Cart

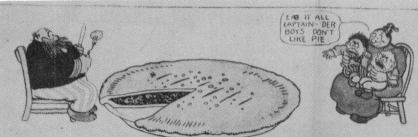

COMIC SUPPLEMENT OF THE
Chicago Sunday AMERICAN
JUNE 19th 1904
COPYRIGHT 1904. BY THE AMERICAN-JOURNAL-EXAMINER
ALL BRITAIN RIGHTS RESERVED.

The Captain Guards the Pies!

"The Captain and the Kids" (1917)

Shortly before the First World War, the Gong Bell Toy Company introduced the "Captain and the Kids" cast-iron bell ringer. As the toy is pulled, Fritz moves back and forth, causing the tiny bell he is holding to ring. The Captain is painted with his blue sailor suit, while Hans and Fritz have yellow pants and red jackets. The Gong Bell Toy Company was one of the great innovators of clever and attractive toys. Their "Captain and the Kids" toy would have to rate as one of their best toys.

A cast-iron toy that depicts two figures on a seesaw, riding on a three-wheel base, is often referred to as a Katzenjammer inspired toy. However, the toy bears no resemblance to any of the Katzenjammer characters and was not originally sold as such.

Today, after 77 years, Hans and Fritz are alive and doing well in the comic strips.

Mamma Katzenjammer bank

Captain and the Kids bell ringer

Seeing New York and Sight Seeing Auto

Katzenjammer Donkey Cart or spanking toy

HAPPY HOOLIGAN

Happy Hooligan is the eternal butt and the most famous of all scapegoats. Happy is jostled by passers-by, arrested and beaten by the police, disclaimed by "decent folks," and scorned and abused by animals. From Happy's efforts to do others a good turn come his misfortunes. His good nature, however, is as unchanging through all this as is the red, tin can hat he's been wearing since his introduction in 1899.

An example of one of Happy's misfortunes is shown in the 1911 Kenton Toy Company's Happy Hooligan Police Patrol. This 17½" long, cast-iron toy has an animated cop who beats Happy over the head with a club as the toy is pulled along. The wagon is yellow with gold trim, red wheels, and black horses. Happy is painted with a green jacket, black pants, red vest, and tin can hat. The cop and the driver, Gloomy Gus, have blue clothing and black hats.

Gus, Happy's brother, was another of Frederick Opper's great creations, who occasionally appeared along with Happy Hooligan in the strip. Gloomy Gus in a cart was marketed by the Harris Toy Company in 1903. This cast-iron toy is over 7" long and painted in bright colors. Happy was also made by Harris in the same horse cart. Both figures are removable. Still other variations of Happy and Gus are two slightly different, 14" long horse carts in which each was riding. Another Harris variation is an 18" long, two-horse cart in which both Happy and Gus are riding together.

Happy Hooligan, by Schoenhut

Happy Hooligan Police Patrol

13

The most sought after of all Happy Hooligan toys is the Happy Hooligan Automobile Toy by the N. N. Hill Brass Company of East Hampton, Connecticut. Produced shortly after the turn of the century, this extremely rare toy is highly popular among many toy collectors as it falls into four major categories: cast-iron, bell ringer, automotive, and, of course, comic strip character. It's made of cast-iron and measures 6″ long and 5″ high. The bell, which is under the floorboard, rings as the toy moves. The car resembles a very large homemade soapbox auto. The old-fashioned dark lamp on the front is sitting on a box which says "soap" on its sides. A chimney coming out of the back seems to indicate the possibility of a steam engine. Perhaps this was Happy's answer to the Stanley Steamer. The car is painted red, while Happy has a yellow jacket and blue pants.

Other horse drawn, Happy Hooligan inspired toys included a 1911 Kenton 6½″ long, cast-iron, horse drawn cart, which came with interchangeable heads for the driver. The oversized heads included Happy, Foxy Grandpa, and Alphonse from Opper's equally immortal strip, "Alphonse and Gaston." The heads are suspended by a short rod which fits into the neck of the driver. This allows the heads to nod back and forth as the toy is moved. The toy is brown with red wheels, while the heads are painted in natural colors. Appropriately, the toy was named "The Nodder" and "Rubber Neck." This minor variation is easily noted, as the name is embossed on both sides of the horse blanket. There are also 11½″ and 17″ fancier models with no names on them.

In 1924, the Schoenhut Toy Company, famous for its jointed, wooden circus toys, also produced Happy as a lovable looking doll. From the color of the clothes to his undersized upper lip, Schoenhut was able to capture the true character of Happy. During the same period Schoenhut also produced a smaller Happy Hooligan on a ladder.

The last of the Happy Hooligan toys was produced in 1932 by the Chein Toy Company. It is a 6″ high, lithographed tin wind-up which waddles along when wound. Happy even has his name on his tin can hat.

Walking Happy Hooligan, by Chein

Gloomy Gus in a Cart

14

Happy Hooligan Nodder in a Cart

H 9348—"Happy Hooligan" Mechanical Toy, 6 inches high. This favorite character is dressed in felt in appropriate colors and walks about in a most comical manner. He will undoubtedly be as popular in a mechanical toy as he has been with the Sunday Supplement reader. Operated by a spring which is wound up by attached thumb piece. Shipping weight, 8 oz. Each ....45c.

Happy Hooligan Automobile Toy

Poor Happy is off to jail again

FOXY GRANDPA

Foxy Grandpa, created by Carl Schultze, began in the *New York Herald* on January 7, 1900. It was a popular children's strip about the adventures of the youthful Foxy Grandpa. In its early days, it rivaled "Buster Brown" and "The Katzenjammer Kids." Schultze went by the pseudonym of "Bunny." The strip lost its popularity after World War I and was discontinued in 1927.

A number of popular toys were inspired by Foxy Grandpa. One of the earliest is a hand-painted, hand-soldered, tin wind-up of Foxy. Its action allows him to simultaneously raise and lower his arms while inching his way across the floor by opening and closing his legs. The toy was manufactured in Germany shortly after the turn of the century.

The single-headed Kenton nodders were mentioned with the Happy Hooligan toy. However, there is a very rare, double-headed, 16" Kenton nodder that employs both Happy and Foxy. The driver is Gloomy Gus. The toy pictured has an Alphonse head on Happy's body, which is incorrect.

Foxy was also made as a small still bank which measures about 5" high. The bank is painted in life-like colors and is fairly easy to find today.

A small, cast-iron bell ringer depicts Foxy as driving a cart with two children pulling it. Foxy's name is embossed on the side of the cart. The toy was hand painted.

Another Foxy toy allows children to try their skill at putting Foxy's hat on his head. By pushing a lever, the hat flips up to his head. The hat is tin and Foxy is cast iron.

Foxy was also employed as the driver of 7" and 14" cast-iron carts. These toys were manufactured by Harris around 1903.

Foxy Grandpa bell ringer

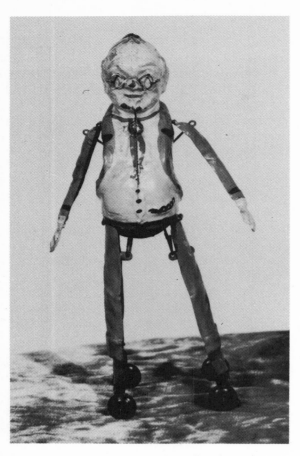

Foxy Grandpa still bank

Early hand-painted Foxy Grandpa

Double-headed Nodder

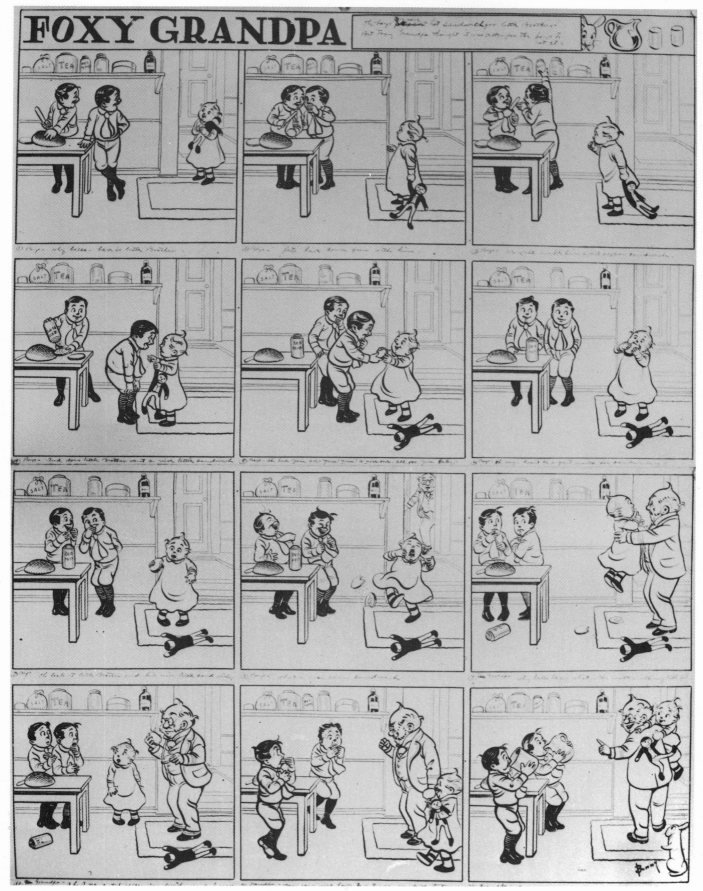

Foxy Grandpa Nodder

Foxy Grandpa Flip the Hat

ALPHONSE and GASTON

Alphonse and Gaston, two of Opper's immortal characters, became national celebrities whose names stood for unbounded politeness and good qualities. Through their incessant bowing and exaggerated manners, these two Frenchmen were able to turn what was well-intentioned politeness into catastrophe.

There were three toys which came from the "Alphonse and Gaston" strip. Two were the "Rubber Neck" and "The Nodders", which were mentioned with the Happy Hooligan toys. Actually, few collectors would actively seek both variations since they are basically identical toys. Collectors should examine this type of toy carefully when buying, as the heads have been recast several times in the last fifteen years. There has also been a recast made of one of the carts. It is simply embossed "Nodders" rather than "The Nodders." The recast heads and carts are almost always aged.

The third toy is the 1911 Kenton "Alphonse and Gaston Auto." This cast-iron toy car measures 8" long and is painted yellow and orange with gold trim. Alphonse and Gaston are animated, as they would take turns bowing as the car moved. It was really quite an ingenious way to illustrate what they will always be remembered for — politeness.

Alphonse Rubber Neck

Alphonse and Gaston Auto

*"Happy Hooligan" and friends — notice the
politeness of Alphonse and Gaston*

BUSTER BROWN

In 1902, Outcault reincarnated his Yellow Kid, only this time in much better social surroundings. With long, golden locks of hair and strictly Victorian clothing, Buster Brown and his faithful, talking bulldog, Tige, retained much of the sardonic style of Outcault, but presented it in a manner much more acceptable to the majority of the American public. Buster was just as mischievous as his predecessor, even though he was well-bred and able to present Outcault's humor in a beguiling manner. At the end of each strip was a moral for Buster, as well as the reader. Although Buster Brown and Tige dropped out of the funny pages after World War I, they are still employed selling children's shoes and clothes today.

Buster and Tige were first sold as a toy only a few years after the strip made its appearance. The toy depicts Tige pulling a small cart in which Buster is riding. It is made entirely of cast iron in a two-piece casting and measures 7½" long. It is painted all silver, as some early iron toys were. Undoubtedly the production of this toy was short-lived and came to a halt when the more attractive, hand-painted, smaller version hit the market. This would help account for the extreme rarity of this toy today.

The hand-painted variation is a completely different toy, not simply a paint variation. It measures over 6" long. Both Buster and Tige are cast iron, while the cart is mostly sheet metal. By careful examination, you can see the many differences in casting in both Buster and Tige.

During the same period, two different Buster Brown and Tige still banks were introduced. They measure about 4" high and were produced in great quantity. There was also a mechanical bank, manufactured by the Stevens Company in 1906, called the "Shoot the Chute Bank," which employed two figures that were unmistakably Buster Brown and Tige. It's a triangular bank with a short extension at the top. Buster and Tige are in a boat which slides down the chute. The bank is finished mostly in silver and is about 12" high.

Early Buster Brown in a Cart

Later painted Buster Brown in a Cart

UNCLE WIGGILY

One of children's best loved animal characters is Uncle Wiggily. Howard Garis conceived his long-eared friend in the early 1900s. Since that time, Uncle Wiggily has entertained millions of children through his adventures in the animal world. He still remains a popular character in children's games and stories. However, Uncle Wiggily's adventures were not always restricted to story books. He also appeared as a daily comic strip in the 1930s, first appearing in the *Evening News* of Newark, New Jersey.

Uncle Wiggily was first manufactured as a toy in the early 1920s as Uncle Wiggily's Crazy Car. The car was made in Germany and is almost 10″ long. It is a tin wind-up, lithographed in a wide variety of different shades of Easter colors. The action of the toy shows Uncle Wiggily jerking to and fro in the driver's seat as the car travels in all different directions. Wiggily is carrying a small valise, with his initials, and his red, white, and blue crutch.

The other Uncle Wiggily toy is also a tin crazy car. However, this Marx version is much easier to find than its rare German counterpart. The car is the same as Charlie McCarthy's, with a minor change in the driver's compartment, different lithographing, and, of course, a different driver. The action of the toy allows the front end to go up and down as the car travels on a wild course and Wiggily's head turns round and round. It carries a 1935 copyright date.

Uncle Wiggily Car, by Marx

Uncle Wiggily German Car

Mutt and Jeff metal, jointed figures

MUTT and JEFF

Bud Fisher, creator of "Mutt and Jeff", got his start as a sports cartoonist, as did Goldberg, Edson, Opper, and others. In 1907, he created a tall, slender, race horse player, who was always on the verge of hitting the big one but was eternally broke. His name was Augustus Mutt. A year later, Mutt was joined by a pint-sized gentleman with a black, silk top hat who had a mustache that ran from ear to ear. His name was Jeff. Mutt was a married man with a son, whereas Jeff was single and carefree. The two have been the closest of friends for almost seventy years. In the beginning, Mutt dominated his small friend and often took advantage of him. Through the years, however, Jeff's incredible endurance has seemed to wear Mutt down.

Not long after the two began running together in the strips, a small cast-iron Mutt and Jeff still bank was produced. It was manufactured for a number of years and is relatively easy to find today.

After World War II, a pair of metal, ball-jointed figures were manufactured in Switzerland. Their feet, hands, and heads are made of plaster while their clothes are felt. Mutt measures 8" tall and Jeff is 6½" tall.

No. 5535

No. 5535—Mechanical Mutt and Jeff. Made of sheet steel, finished in bright colors. Fitted with steel spring. Packed one in a carton.
.................................Per doz. $8.75

Ad for Mechanical Mutt and Jeff

Mutt and Jeff still bank

In the 1920s a small, German, lithographed tin wind-up of Mutt and Jeff was marketed. Jeff is sitting on Mutt's back and facing to the rear.

When Bud Fisher died in 1954, his long-time assistant, Al Smith, continued the strip. Mutt and Jeff's ageless brand of humor has continued to entertain millions of Americans today, as it has for several generations.

"Mutt and Jeff" (1911)

27

BRINGING UP FATHER

Maggie and Jiggs have been in the funny pages over sixty years, a distinction held by only two other comic strips. George McManus, who physically resembled Jiggs, created his colorful couple in 1913 in "Bringing Up Father". It was fashioned after an 1890s play named *The Rising Generation*, which showed the effects of sudden wealth on a workingman's family. "Bringing Up Father" is about Maggie's adventures in high society and Jigg's longing for the poolroom, card games, and, of course, Dinty Moore's, where the room is filled with the fragrance of steaming corned beef and cabbage.

Looking through some of McManus's earlier strips, glimpses of Jiggs are visible: bullet-shaped head, long round jaw, and button nose. By ingeniously using the angle of the mouth and level of the eyebrows, McManus was able to show a magnitude of emotions.

The Maggie and Jiggs tin wind-up was one of several variations of similar toys manufactured in the 1920s by Nifty, a German toy company. The basic principle behind the toy is a clockwork mechanism under one end, which makes the toy stop and start and go backwards and forwards. The two ends of the toy are connected by a thin 2" strip of spring steel which forces the figures to jump back and forth at each other, due to its quick and jerky movements. Under the opposite end of the wind-up mechanism is an axle that slides back and forth on one side and allows the toy to go in erratic directions. This adds to the excitement, making the toy more realistic, as if a real fight were going on. The overall length is 7".

Maggie and Jiggs are full figures, lithographed in bright colors. Jiggs has a cane in one hand, while Maggie has a rolling pin. Jiggs's bright red nose and tranquil smile seem to indicate that he is returning home from a night at Dinty Moore's. From Maggie's terrifying frown and attack-like stance, we know what her intent is. She even has her pet dog after Jiggs.

Another clever lithographed tin wind-up from Nifty was Jiggs In His Jazz Car. Jiggs's head would turn from side to side as the car traveled in a circular direction. The toy measures 6½" long and is very difficult to find today. It was marketed in 1924.

During the same period, Schoenhut produced their dressed, wood-jointed dolls of Maggie and Jiggs. Maggie, of course, is holding her rolling pin, and Jiggs a bucket of corned beef and cabbage.

When George McManus died in 1954, a true giant in cartooning was gone. "Bringing Up Father", however, was far too popular to discontinue and was carried on by others.

Jiggs in his Jazz Car

Maggie and Jiggs, by Schoenhut

Maggie and Jiggs tin wind-up

Five metal Toonerville Trolleys

THE TOONERVILLE TROLLEY

The everyday events of a diversified cast of characters and one old, decrepit-looking trolley were the basic theme of one of the best loved and remembered of all comic strips, "The Toonerville Trolley That Meets All Trains." In his cartoons, creator Fontaine Fox recorded that colorful era in American history after the turn of the century. A run-down old trolley which Fox and his wife once rode in Pelham, New York, along with an equally dilapidated trolley in his home town of Louisville, Kentucky, served as the prototypes of his Toonerville Trolley. Even his characters were modeled after boyhood chums and other people he had known.

Fox created the world of a golden age in American history and shared it with us for over 40 years. In 1955, the Toonerville folks had reached the end of the line. Fontaine Fox retired. Since Fox was one of the few artists who owned his own strip, he was able to retire his Toonerville Folks when he did.

Today, "Toonerville Trolley" inspired toys are enthusiastically sought after by almost all toy collectors. The most familiar toy is the tin, wind-up Toonerville Trolley manufactured by Nifty in 1922. This 5″ long, 7″ high toy has one of the more intricate clockwork mechanisms and amusing actions of any toy manufactured after the turn of the century. When wound, it proceeds forward in a rocking motion, due to an eccentric rear wheel. After the trolley has advanced several feet, it stops and begins shaking as the Skipper feverishly turns the controller. A few seconds later, it's back on its way again.

2F7009 — "Katrinka," "Jimmy" and wheelbarrow, 6¾ in. high, red and blue lithographed, Katrinka raises and lowers Jimmy in wheelbarrow, then moves on. ¹⁄₁₂ doz. in box. Doz. **$8.00**

Ad for Katrinka, Jimmy, and Wheelbarrow

30

The identical Toonerville Trolley also came in two lesser-known variations. The first has wheels made to run on tracks, which came with that model. The second variation employs a simple barrel spring, which didn't allow for the intricate comical movements of the clockwork trolley. Also, the Skipper is attached by a small spring on his feet.

Another one of Nifty's ingenious toys was The Powerful Katrinka. In Fox's strip, Katrinka was renowned for her extraordinary strength. Appropriately, Nifty displayed her famed strength by having her raise and lower a young lad named Jimmy.

There are two variations of The Powerful Katrinka. In one variation, she pushes Jimmy along in a wheelbarrow, stops, raises and lowers the wheelbarrow, and starts on her way again. In the other variation, she simply scurries along, raising and lowering Jimmy with one hand. The Powerful Katrinka is 5½" high and copyrighted 1923.

Produced during the same period was Fox's Immortal Aunt Eppie Hogg, "the fastest woman in three counties." Eppie is on the rear end of a 7" long, green truck. The truck is driven by The Skipper, the conductor of the Toonerville Trolley. Unfortunately, he is missing from the toy pictured. Often figures attached by means of small tabs, as was the Skipper, are missing. The action of this toy is quite unique. As the truck travels along, Eppie begins to slide off the rear end. As the front end flies up, she begins to slide back on the truck. The front end again falls to the floor, and the truck starts on its way.

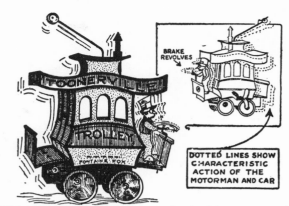

2F7010—"Toonerville Trolley," 6¾ in. high, bright colored. When wound the "Skipper" motor man starts and stops car in life-like manner and car moves with characteristic action, strong spring. 1/12 doz. in box. Doz **$8.00**

Ad for Toonerville Trolley

Aunt Eppie Hogg on a Truck

Tin, wind-up Toonerville Trolley

In 1929, Dent Hardware Company of Fullerton, Pennsylvania, began producing a cast-iron model of the Toonerville Trolley. Its appearance is quite similar to the tin wind-up. This model is made in a two-piece casting, with the Skipper fitting loosely in a notch in the floor board. Two eccentric wheels cause the trolley to sway from side to side while crossing the floor. It was made in two color variations: green with orange trim, and red with yellow trim. Both have gold paint applied to the raised letters and edges of the platforms. The cast-iron Toonerville is 4" long and 6" high.

Several years ago, about 20 cast iron Toonervilles came on the toy market. Each appeared brand new, as they had been recently painted. It seems that a small number of unpainted, unassembled, rejected parts had supposedly been saved along with other scrap iron at the Dent factory many years ago. Fortunately, the rejected parts were never sold as scrap iron and they eventually found their way into the hands of a toy collector. Even though these newly assembled and painted Toonervilles are supposedly made from old parts they are far less desirable or valuable than an old original manufactured iron Toonerville. As with any repainted iron toy they can be dinged up to give an old appearance. However,

HO-Gauge Toonerville Trolley

Both variations of the Powerful Katrinka

close inspection should reveal the age of the paint to a knowledgeable toy collector.

A crude looking Toonerville with the Skipper and a lady passenger was produced in pot metal. The toy carries a 1923 copyright and "F Fox" on one side. This 4" high toy comes in three different color variations, red, green, and yellow, all with different colored trim.

By the late 1930s, an HO gauge electric Toonerville Trolley was available to railroad buffs. This 2½" high trolley, manufactured by Kemtron Products Company by agreement with Fontaine Fox, came complete with a tiny working headlight. This trolley was made mostly of brass and sold unpainted.

During the 1920s and 1930s, there were a number of small, wooden, jointed comic strip characters manufactured. Some were dressed figures, while most were only painted. One wind-up wood figure was Mickey McGuire, the cigar-smoking young ruffian from the Toonerville Trolley. Mickey was also a dressed figure.

The smallest of the Toonerville Trolleys, referred to by most collectors as the Tin Miniature Toonerville Trolley, is slightly less than 2" high and 1½" long. It remains a mystery whether this German miniature was marketed, a Crackerjacks toy, or a giveaway. Regardless, it is a highly prized toy. It carries a 1922 copyright, along with its originator's name, Fontaine Fox.

Mickey McGuire wooden, dressed wind-up

Tin, miniature Toonerville Trolley

Pot metal Toonerville Trolley

"Toonerville Folks" (1928)

CHARLIE CHAPLIN

Charlie Chaplin, known to millions as the "Little Tramp," brought the gift of laughter to the world. He was born to parents in the theatrical profession. At an early age, he and his brother Sydney joined a vaudeville troupe. He came to America in 1910 as the leading comedian of the Karno Comedy Company and played in vaudeville until 1913, when he joined the Keystone Studio.

His first appearance, as the villain of a one-reel comedy, was the forerunner of the character that would distinguish him throughout the world. By the time he made his second film, his screen character was complete with over-sized shoes, baggy trousers, derby hat, cane, and mustache.

Charlie Chaplin was a genius in his field. He prepared his own stories and directed them. By 1918, Charlie and his brother formed their own studio, the Charlie Chaplin Film Company.

Chaplin was an ideal subject for a comic strip. The character was ready-made and instantly recog-

Charlie Chaplin on a Bicycle

Charlie Chaplin squeeze toy

nizable. It first appeared in 1915 and continued to run for several years. The strip was drawn by several cartoonists, among them Elzie Segar of "Popeye" fame, Ed Carey, and Gus Mager.

The spirit of comedy and pathos of the "Little Tramp" were also captured in the toys made to emulate him. Perhaps the most widely known of all the Chaplin toys is the 8¾" high, lithographed tin wind-up with cast-iron feet. Charlie rocks back and forth at the waist, which gives him the appearance of walking in his famous shuffling manner. The toy was marketed just prior to 1920 and was not marked by the manufacturer.

The Charlie Chaplin dancing toy was also marketed just prior to 1920. It is a 5½" by 7" paper-covered tin box which allowed the Chaplin figure to move up and down. His jointed legs make him appear to be dancing.

During the 1920s, a small German squeeze toy was marketed. It is lithographed tin and shows Charlie holding a cat and a cymbal. When the plunger is

pushed, his arm rises and the cymbals strike.

A small, French-looking Chaplin made of wood, metal, and cloth, was imported in the early twenties. Whether it was originally sold as Charlie Chaplin is not known. However, the resemblance is unmistakable, and how it was originally sold seems to be of little importance, because today's antique toy collectors have accepted it as Charlie Chaplin.

Another unmistakable Chaplin toy depicts Charlie as a bike rider. The 8" long, lithographed tin bike was made to balance on a string. When one end of the string is lifted, Charlie will pedal vigorously to the other end. This clever toy was also manufactured with several other figures.

Chaplin was used as the figure on a bell ringer, which was made prior to 1920. Charlie is painted cast iron, while the rest of the toy is made of sheet metal.

Another of the more widely known Chaplin toys is the 6½" high, Schuco Charlie Chaplin. Charlie shuffles along while spinning his cane. The toy, which is made of tin, is fully dressed with a felt covering on the face.

Schuco, a German toy company, did manufacture one other Chaplin toy. It is, perhaps, the rarest of all the Chaplin toys. It was called the Charlie Chaplin Boxer-Champion. The toy is similar to the other Chaplin toy except for his dress and its boxing action. The inspiration for the toy came from a movie Chaplin starred in, called *The Champion*. In the movie, Charlie became a champion boxer through some hilarious circumstances and with the help of a dog named Spike.

Charlie Chaplin Spinning the Cane

Charlie Chaplin Boxer-Champion

Tin, wind-up Charlie Chaplin (cast-iron feet)

Charlie Chaplin bell ringer

Charlie Chaplin (French)

Charlie Chaplin Dancing

"Charlie Chaplin" (1915)

KRAZY KAT

Krazy, Ignatz, and Offisa B Pupp, symbols of our most influential human forces, were portrayed on the surrealistic backdrop of desert country in Arizona. Krazy loves Ignatz and receives the blow of Ignatz's omnipresent brick as an arrow from Cupid's bow. Ignatz is regulated in his disdain and uncontrollable fury for everything in nature by Offisa B. Pupp, whose feelings for Krazy are unequalled, perfect love.

The genius of George Herriman created this strange love triangle. His artistry was revolutionary in the comic strips. Frames jumped from day to night for no apparent reason, the frames appeared in no orderly sequence, and his deft use of color assembled the unit as a whole. Herriman's first work was published in 1901. He experimentally placed Krazy between the floorboards of his major strip, "The Family Upstairs." A month after Krazy appeared, it became an independent strip and launched a rewarding career that would span 28 years.

The two tin toys which were made of Krazy were both variations of Felix the Cat toys. Krazy Kat on a scooter is a lithographed tin wind-up made by Nifty around 1930. Krazy is black with a white face and ribbon, and his name appears on his tail. The body of the scooter is orange and the wheels are green. When wound up, Krazy jumps up and down as the toy runs in circles. Overall dimensions are 8″ by 6½″.

The other toy induces action as it is pulled. Krazy is chasing two yellow and red mice on a platform. The mice look suspiciously like twin Ignatzes. The platform is orange with green wheels, is 7½″ long, and contains a noisemaker. Again it is lithographed tin made by Nifty in the early 1930s. Krazy is black with a white face and ribbon and looks essentially the same as Krazy on the scooter, except that his name appears on both sides of his body. Both "Kats" have moon-shaped eyes characteristic of the early Mickey Mouse.

Herriman provided his fans with an unorderly fantasy, heavily laced with poetry on the theme of Krazy's unabashed love. This intimacy ended with Herriman's death in 1944. His editors were wise to decide that a successor could never equal the genius of George Herriman.

Krazy Kat on a Scooter

Ad for Krazy Kat Chasing Mice

Krazy Kat platform toy

Very early "Krazy Kat"

THE GUMPS

Andy Gump, one of the most unusual looking characters in the history of comic strips, made his first appearance in the *Chicago Tribune* in 1917. The publisher, Captain Joseph Patterson, conceived and named his chinless protege and family, "The Gumps." However, the actual cartooning was left to one of his staff cartoonists, Sidney Smith.

By the 1920s, "The Gumps" had become the most popular family strip of the day. "The Gumps" undoubtedly had little meaning to the people who made the twenties famous: the gangsters, flappers and high society. It was meaningful, however, to that majority of just plain common folk. To them, "The Gumps" represented bread, potatoes, near-beer, and the age-old process of trying to get ahead.

In 1924, the Arcade Manufacturing Company began producing Andy Gump in his 348 car. Arcade produced three variations of this cast-iron toy. The first was the cheapest model and has a nickle-plated figure, wheels, and a 348 grill. The car itself is bright red. The second model is more ornate, having a painted figure with predominately green clothing. The center section of the wheels is also painted green with a red hub. The deluxe model was the third and last. Andy is painted in more diversified colors with a dark blue suit. The wheels on the car are white with a green center and red hubs. The red body of the car is trimmed in green, and the 348 grill is painted silver with the raised numbers painted black. This model is equipped with a rear 348 plate, which is also painted like the front grill, and a red crank. The overall dimensions of the car are 6″ high and 7¼″ long.

During the same period, Arcade also produced Andy's son, Chester, in a cast-iron pony cart. Chester is in lifelike colors, and the cart is yellow with red wheels and a white horse. The overall dimensions are 4½″ high by 8″ long.

Due to the popularity of both Andy and Chester, most of these toys saw a great many hours of play. Both figures are removable, as are Andy's grill, crank, and rear plate. Consequently, the toys are sometimes found in an incomplete state (if, indeed, you are lucky enough to find one at all). The paint chipped easily, as with all cast-iron toys. As a result, very few deluxe models are to be found today with more than half of the white enamel on the wheels. Few mint examples of these toys survive. However, most toy collectors would be glad to add either Andy or Chester to their collection in almost any reasonable condition.

During the 1920s, Arcade also made a 4½″ high, Andy Gump still bank. The bank depicts Andy sitting on a tree stump. He appears to be holding something in his hands, but whether he originally came with something is a point of dispute among many bank collectors. Andy has a tan suit and gloves, brown hat, white shirt, blue tie, and black shoes. The bank is a two-piece casting held together by a screw in Andy's side.

In 1932, the Tootsietoy Company manufactured a set of six different miniature, pot metal, comic strip character toys, which included Andy Gump in his 348 car. The boxed sets were hand-painted with as many as seven different colors being used on each toy. These are action toys with a cam on the rear axle pushing the figure up and down. The average length of these toys is 2¾″. The boxed sets of six sold for one dollar. They were also sold separately in a non-action, simple color scheme variation at ten cents each. In 1933, Tootsietoy discontinued their production as they were a financial failure. Today these clever toys are the most sought after of all the Tootsietoys. The complete series included: Andy Gump in his 348 car; Moon Mullins in a police patrol; Kayo in an ice truck; Uncle Willie and Mamie in a boat; Uncle Walt in a roadster; and Smitty and Herby on a sidecar motorcycle.

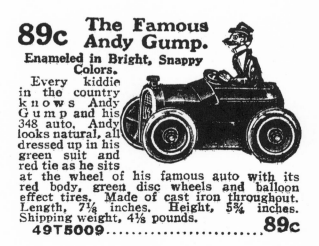

Ad for Andy Gump and his 348 auto

Andy Gump in his 348 car (nickle-plated figure)

Andy Gump 348 Car, by Tootsietoy

Andy Gump in his 348 car (deluxe model)

Andy Gump still bank

Small, wooden, jointed Andy Gump

Chester Gump Pony Cart

BOOB McNUTT

Rube Goldberg, remembered by many for his wildly complicated inventions, was one of the most colorful of all cartoonists. He started out as a sports cartoonist, shortly after the turn of the century. Before he was 25, he had become a recognized artist and writer. He had also become a gambling czar, which was due mainly to an old boxing rule that did not allow for a referee's decision in fights that ended without a knockout. Instead, all bets were settled according to the decision of the sports page writers and cartoonists.

By 1915, Goldberg's reputation was renowned. His cartoons of "Mike and Ike the Look Alike Boys", "Foolish Questions", "They All Look Alike When You're Far Away", and others, had practically become the heart of the now defunct New York paper called the *Evening Mail*.

Around 1918, with the help of a couple of friends, Goldberg became syndicated under the new McNaught Syndicate. One of their first new strips was about the adventures of a sad looking young man with red hair, whose tiny hat fit him as poorly as did the rest of his clothes. Boob was a good-hearted fellow who always wanted to help but got himself in trouble doing it.

In 1925, the Ferdinand Strauss Corporation first marketed the tin lithographed wind-up of Boob McNutt. He measures 9″ tall and walks along with a shaking motion when wound. There are two variations of the Boob McNutt toy itself: one depicted him exactly as he looked in the strip; the other employed a large hat which allowed Boob to perform on his head.

On a few occasions, a couple of toy companies used patterns and parts made by a different company when manufacturing several of their toys. How the details of these transactions were worked out is not fully known. A classic example is shown by comparing the Strauss Boob McNutt to the Marx Hey Hey Chicken Snatcher. Both are identical, other than the addition of the dog and the chicken to the Marx toy and, of course, a completely different lithographing. There were other lithographing variations of Boob McNutt, none of which are comic strip characters. Both Boob's name and his creator's name were signed on his back.

In the early 1920s, the Schoenhut Company produced a wooden, jointed Boob McNutt. He is about 9″ tall and came in cloth clothes and a tiny, wooden hat.

By 1934, Goldberg retired Boob in order to devote more of his time to writing. Goldberg, at the age of eighty, developed a new career for himself in the field of sculpturing. He even designed the "Reuben Award," given to the outstanding cartoonist of the year by The National Cartoonist Society. Rube Goldberg died in 1970, at the age of 87.

F3268 — "Boob McNutt," 9½ in. high, red, black and black and yellow figure, replica of famous comic character. Dances and performs on head. ¼ doz. in in pkg. Doz **$4.35**

Boob McNutt tin wind-up, by Strauss

Hey Hey the Chicken Snatcher, by Marx

Boob McNutt, by Schoenhut

Boob McNutt

"Boob McNutt" (1921)

TOOTS AND CASPER

Jimmy Murphy's "Toots and Casper" was perhaps the most exaggerated of all family strips. Casper was a well meaning boob of a husband. Toots, Casper's wife, was a beautiful young woman who could have undoubtedly done better than Casper but loved him just the same. Buttercup, their beloved baby, ruled the roost and furnished the comedy that made the strip hilariously funny. Buttercup made his debut a few years after the strip was started in 1918. Their dog was named Spare Ribs. The "Toots and Casper" strip was so popular that a movie was made in 1928, based on the strip.

Both of the "Toots and Casper" inspired toys are extremely hard to find today. One is an 8″ long, lithographed tin, animated pull toy. It was manufactured by Nifty in the mid 1920s. When the toy is pulled, Buttercup appears to be hitting Spare Ribs with a small broom. At the same time, Spare Ribs' head goes up and down as if he were trying to get away.

The other toy was called The Crawling Buttercup. It is a hand-painted, tin wind-up which measures 8″ long and 5″ high. This truly unique toy uses its arms and legs to crawl, while its head turns from side to side. Its doll-like characteristics would seem to make it an appealing toy to doll collectors also. A tag around his neck carries Buttercup's name as well as the creator's name. The toy is marked Germany but carries no manufacturer's name.

Crawling Buttercup

Buttercup and Spare Ribs platform toy

'Toots and Casper' (1928)

BETTY BOOP

Betty Boop was a young lady who first found success in animated movie cartoons, then comic strips, and later television. Her creator, Max Fleischer, was one of the founding fathers of animated cartoons. The comic strip depicted Betty as a movie queen.

In the 1930s, she was produced as a 7″ high, celluloid figure on a tin base. A pendulum-type rod behind her back allowed her head to rock from side to side.

BARNEY GOOGLE

The 1920s and 1930s are often referred to as the golden years of the comic strip. One character who probably did as much as anyone to help create that image was a small saucer-eyed, potato-nosed, tin-horn gambler named Barney Google. Barney was the con man who never quite made it. Faced with the worldly problems of rent, job, prestige, and general responsibility, he meets one crisis after another while always seeming to be on the edge of disaster. However, Barney Google's cheerful belief that he could someday straighten everything out endeared him to millions of readers.

Billy DeBeck, a small man himself, soon realized he had the makings of a great cartoon after Barney began running in the papers in 1919. But something seemed to be missing, a companion for Barney. In 1922, DeBeck set the stage for the entrance of Barney's new friend, Sparkplug. Barney, while standing outside a saloon, quite accidently broke the fall of a race horse owner, who was being ejected from a first floor window. In return for the favor, Barney was presented with a two year old race horse named Sparkplug. Public reaction was so overwhelming that Billy Rose wrote a song called "Barney Google with the Goo-Goo-Googly Eyes."

Sparkplug possessed the same saucer-shaped eyes as his owner. His oversized horse blanket helped to make an already ridiculous looking horse even more absurd. Another one of Barney's friends was his troublesome ostrich, Rudy. Rudy managed to keep Barney in continuous trouble for many years. Other friends included Barney's Negro jockey, Sunshine; his girlfriend, Sweet Mamma; and Sully, the strong man.

In 1934, the strip changed. Barney and Sully, forced to leave town, headed south. There they met Snuffy Smith and family, hillbillies of the purer variety. Snuffy, who physically resembled Barney, became very popular. Years later, he managed to take over the strip.

The most widely known of the Barney Google toys is the early 1920s Barney Google Riding Sparkplug. It is a lithographed tin wind-up which measures 7½" high and 7½" long. As the toy moves forward, Barney jumps up and down and Sparkplug's head and tail go up and down. Sparkplug is wearing his patched, old, yellow horse blanket, which carries a 1924 copyright. The toy was manufactured by Nifty. Collectors should pay careful attention to Barney's hat brim when inspecting this toy. Because it fit loosely to begin with, it is often missing or replaced.

Rudy was also manufactured by Nifty during the same period. This quite scarce, tin toy is 9" tall and has a lithographed body while the tail, neck, head, legs, and feet are hand-painted. Several German, lithographed tin toys manufactured during this period were hand-painted in certain areas with touch-up paint when the toy was completely assembled.

Barney Google and Spark Plug, by Schoenhut

The touched up areas oftentimes crack and flake off with age, while the lithographed areas remain bright. Collectors should use extreme care when cleaning hand-painted areas.

Another rare tin lithographed toy features Barney, Sparky, and Sunshine. Barney is riding a scooter, while Sunshine is astride Sparkplug. As the toy is pulled, Barney and Sunshine begin racing. One will jump ahead for a second, then fall behind. The toy is called the Barney Google Racing Toy. It measures 8″ long and over 6″ high. The full-figured characters are signed with a 1924 copyright and their creator's name, DeBeck.

Schoenhut came out with beautiful Barney Google and Sparkplug fully dressed, jointed, wood dolls during the latter part of the 1920s. Sparkplug is wearing a yellow horse blanket with his name on it, which buttons up the front. Barney is wearing checked pants and a black jacket. His wooden hat is made to resemble one of his old trade marks, a black silk top hat. It was a luxury he afforded himself when Sparky won his first race. Unfortunately for Barney, it was to be the only race Sparkplug would ever win.

There were also several cheap, wooden toys of Sparkplug manufactured around 1930. The one pictured is about 9″ long. These toys were flat figures, non-mechanical, and unattractive. Consequently, few collectors are interested in them today.

When Billy DeBeck died in 1942, Barney and Snuffy were left in the expert hands of Fred Lasswell, DeBeck's long-time assistant. Today Snuffy is still in the comic strips, but, with most of the original characters gone, something seems to be missing — at least to a nostalgic toy collector.

Rudy the Ostrich

Wooden Spark Plug

2F7002—"Spark Plug" & "Barney Google," 7½ in. high. "Sparky" with yellow blanket, shakes head and wags tail. "Barney" with black coat and blue trousers, goes through the motion of expert rider. Each in box. ¼ doz. in pkg.......Doz **$8.00**

Barney Google and Spark Plug toy

Barney Google Racing Toy

*An early "Barney Google" — Barney's size was
normal at first*

54

"Barney Google" in 1921, one year before Spark Plug — notice how he has become smaller

55

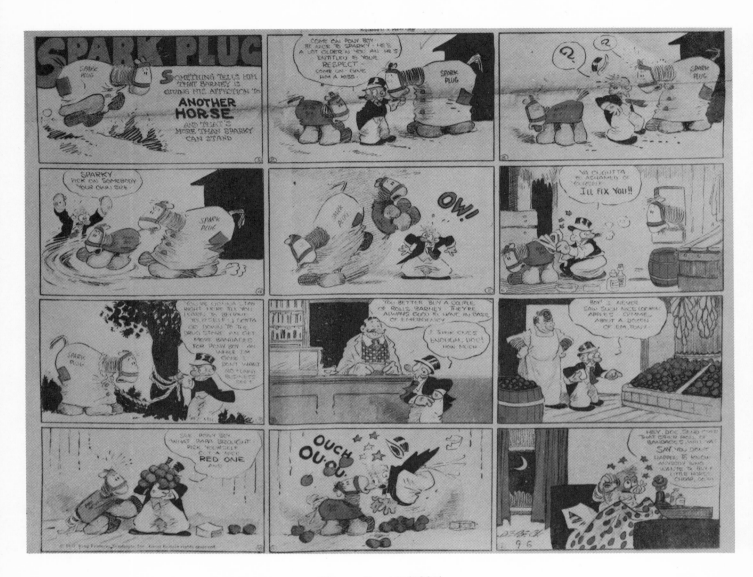

"Barney Google" (1931)

POPEYE

Popeye, one of the most famous of all comic strip characters, was created in 1929. Elzie Segar, Popeye's creator, was a recognized cartoonist long before 1929.

Segar, born in Chester, Illinois, in 1895, began his career working for the *Chicago Herald* under the direction of Richard Outcault, creator of the "The Yellow Kid" and "Buster Brown." By 1917, the *Herald* went out of business, and Segar went to work for the *Chicago American.*

In 1919, Segar's big break came when, on a trip to New York, he presented his proposed Thimble Theatre cartoon to King Features. They liked his new cartoon so well, they immediately drew up a contract.

The Thimble Theatre was based on the adventures of the Oyl family. The love interest revolved around Olive Oyl and her boyfriend, Ham Gravy. Other main characters were: Olive's idiot brother, Castor Oyl; her mother, Nana Oyl; and her father, Cole Oyl. One of the funniest things about the strip was the characters themselves. Well-worn gags coming from such ludicrously original characters could be construed as nothing but humor.

Popeye's introduction came in January, 1929, after the Oyl's had purchased a large boat and suddenly discovered they knew nothing about sailing. Castor was looking along the docks for someone to help them, when he ran across a bell-bottomed, one-eyed sailor, smoking a corn cob pipe. Castor asked, "Hey there! Are you a sailor?" Popeye answered with his first words, "Ja think I'm a cowboy?" At this point, the Thimble Theatre became merely a stage for the adventures of Popeye, and the strip was renamed a few years later.

Two themes shaped the adventures of Popeye. First was his somewhat unusual romance with Olive Oyl. Olive, whose body resembled Andy Gump's or several pipe stems twisted together, somehow managed to attract a steady stream of rivals to Popeye. These rivals, along with the good deeds which the world needs done, created Popeye's role. He became Popeye, the fighting man. He was aided, of course, by his always convenient can of spinach.

Popeye has emerged through the years as a sort of seagoing Lancelot, protector of all that's virtuous. He is ignorant of good manners, swears in public, reads with the ability of a five year old child, but, most important of all, is pure in heart and abundantly generous.

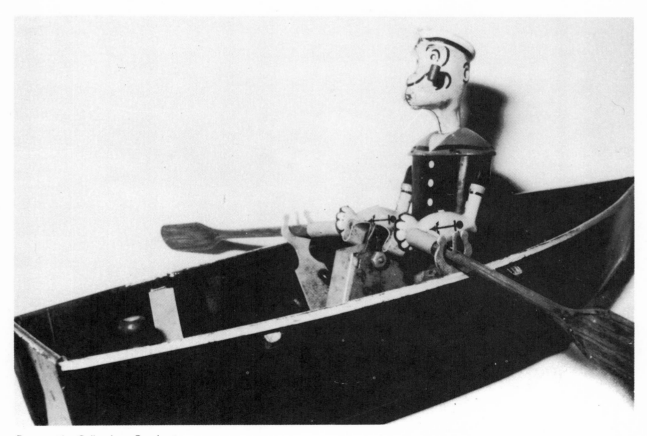

Popeye the Sailor in a Rowboat

Popeye Patrol

Popeye has probably been reproduced in more toys than any other comic strip character, with the possible exception of Mickey Mouse. Oddly enough, the toy which is most characteristic of Popeye is the hardest to find. It is the 15″ long Popeye the Sailor in a Rowboat. It was manufactured in 1935 by the Hoge Manufacturing Company of New York. Its long running, hand-cranked motor allowed Popeye to row in the water for quite a distance. The oars were removable.

Two other very hard to find Popeye toys are the 1938 Hubley cast-iron motorcycles. The smaller one measures 5½″ long and is called the Popeye Spinach Delivery. The figure is of a solid casting and is removable. This motorcycle is seldom found with the original figure. However, the figure has been reproduced.

While the larger motorcycle does not seem to be quite as rare as the smaller one, it is more desirable to most toy collectors and therefore commands a higher price. It is called the Popeye Patrol and measures almost 9″ long. The figure is removable and made in a two-piece casting with solid, cast, jointed arms.

Popeye Spinach Delivery

Also produced in the 1930s was the Marx, lithographed tin Popeye Express that showed Popeye in an airplane. Popeye would fly above, while Olive, Wimpy, Sappo, and Swee' Pea would circle in a train below. It measures over 9″ in diameter. Several similar non-comic strip toys were also made by Marx. While most of them are common today, the Popeye toy is very scarce.

Another Marx toy which employed airplanes is the Popeye Flyer. This same toy was produced without the Popeye lithographing in several variations, also.

The last of the Popeye planes is a 7″ long Popeye The Pilot. The action of the toy caused the plane to go in erratic directions while making sudden starts and stops. There are two variations of this plane. One is shown in the book, while the other has different lithographing and a slightly differently shaped body.

Another Popeye Express, by Marx, is a completely different toy than the one with Popeye in the plane. This one had Popeye pushing a wheel barrow with a trunk on the top. There are two minor variations. One has an animated parrot, which would pop in and out of the trunk while the toy was operating. The parrot was stationary on the other model.

Popeye the Flyer

Popeye the Pilot

Popeye Express

Popeye Express with the Airplane

Popeye and the Parrot Cages

Popeye in a Barrel

Probably the most common of the Popeye toys is Popeye Carrying the Parrot Cages, by Marx. When wound, Popeye would simply walk along in a comical manner.

Chein also made two walking type Popeyes. One measures 6″ high, is lithographed tin, and walks with a shaking motion. The identical toy was also lithographed as Barnical Bill. This, however, is not a comic strip character toy. The other Chein toy is a 7″ Popeye in a Barrel. It is also lithographed tin and operates with a shaking motion.

Two other similar Chein toys were the Popeye and the Punching Bag. The smaller one measured 7½″ high and has the bag coming up from the floor. The larger one was about 10″ high and has an overhead bag. Both were made of lithographed tin with a celluloid bag. Popeye would actually punch the bag when wound.

Another Chein toy was called Popeye The Heavy Hitter. Popeye would raise and drop the mallet, trying to ring the bell. This toy is lithographed tin. Notice the cartoon on the side of the toy.

Popeye and the Overhead Punching Bag

Popeye and the Punching Bag

Walking Popeye, by Chein

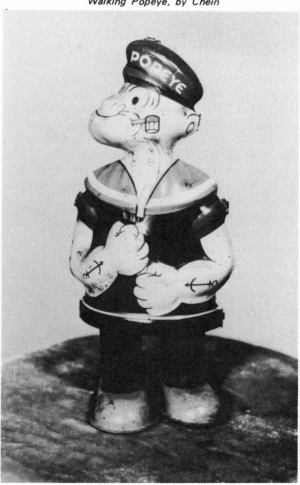

61

Around 1935, Marx marketed their Popeye Handcar. It's a variation of the deluxe Moon Mullins and Kayo Handcar. However, the figures, Popeye and Olive Oyl, were made of rubber. Today this toy is very difficult to find with the figures intact.

In the 1940s, Marx manufactured Popeye The Champ. The toy is lithographed tin while the figures are celluloid. The fast-moving action included a bell that would ring. Popeye was also produced in another boxing toy. It is a small tin bank called the Popeye Knockout Bank and it sold for $.25 in the late 40s and early 50s.

There were two Popeye sparklers. One was a 1930 German sparkler that is shaped like Popeye's head. In 1959, Chein marketed a sparkler which is circular-shaped.

During the mid 1930s, Marx marketed two variations of a Popeye Dancing on the Roof. One had Popeye alone on the roof. The other had Olive Oyl with him. He would dance as she moved from side to side, as if playing the accordian.

Popeye was also manufactured as the driver of a horse-drawn cart. The toy was lithographed tin, except for Popeye, who was celluloid.

Popeye was even made climbing a string. The toy was essentially the same as the climbing monkey toy, except Popeye was the figure on the string.

The early 1960s seemed to be a boom era for Japanese toy makers. A number of tin, wind-up comic strip character toys helped their popularity. The majority of their toys were Walt Disney creations. Line Mar Toys, a subdivision of Marx, was the leader in this area. Pictured is what is considered to be one of the finest of all the Line Mar toys, the Popeye on Roller Skates. It is lithographed tin, except for the cloth pants and wooden pipe. When wound, Popeye actually appears to be roller-skating. The wind-up mechanism is hidden in one leg. There were several other Line Mar Popeye toys.

Few toy collectors who buy the Line Mar toys today actually collect them. Most are simply speculating. As the old comic strip character toys continue to become harder to find, many collectors may begin adding the Japanese Line Mar toys to their older comic strip character toys. Hopefully, their investment will double within a few years.

Popeye's immense popularity brought about an age of Popeye-mania. By 1940, he was on a Navy recruiting poster and reproduced in cakes of soap, cutouts, dolls, candy, toys, and a variety of other items. There was even a monument erected to Popeye in the heart of the spinach region of Texas.

Popeye on Roller Skates, by Line Mar (Japanese)

Popeye Heavy Hitter

Popeye sparkler (1930s)

Small, wooden, jointed Popeye

Popeye sparkler (1959), by Chein

Popeye and Olive Oyl on the Roof

Popeye the Champ

Popeye — one year after his introduction in 1929

64

FELIX THE CAT

Felix sparkler

Felix on a Scooter

"Felix the Cat" began as an animated movie cartoon in 1920. By 1923, Felix had become so popular he was made into a comic strip and was syndicated by King Features. His creator, Pat Sullivan, has been credited by many as being an innovator in depicting motion in the strip. Felix's wanderings through a dream-like world were not always rewarding. Poor Felix usually seemed to receive the worst of things.

Two of the Felix tin toys are simply variations of the two Krazy Kat toys already mentioned. About the only differences were the absence of Krazy's ribbon, Felix's circular eyes, and the different names. The Felix platform toy did not employ a noise maker.

Another Felix tin toy is called the Walking Felix. It is a painted, German, tin wind-up which carries an attached metal band on his chest with his name, copyright dates, and his creator's name. Occasionally the metal band will be missing. The tail is often missing, as is the case with the one pictured.

A walking cat similar to Felix was made in Germany. It had arms that stuck straight out rather than folded behind its back and was sold as "Comical Cat."

A 5″ hand sparkler of Felix was marketed in the 1920s. By pushing the plunger, colored sparks could be seen in Felix's eyes and mouth.

There is a large variety of Felix figures, ranging from jointed, wood dolls to small cast-iron pieces. One of the most unusual ones is a semi-animated, 3″ high, cast-iron Felix with an umbrella. The head is attached by a thin piece of spring steel, which allows Felix to nod his head back and forth. His creator's name is on the bottom of his feet.

Felix platform toy

2F7015—"Felix" the walking cat. Walks with swaying motion of body in characteristic position. Each in box. ¼ doz. in pkg..........Doz **$4.00**

Cast-iron Felix (nodding head)

Walking Felix

GASOLINE ALLEY

Does anyone remember when Skeezix of "Gasoline Alley" was left on Uncle Walt's doorstep? It was Valentine's Day, 1921, and Americans everywhere shifted their attentions from tinkering with the newly popular automobile to watching the week-old Skeezix grow up. "Gasoline Alley" mirrors small town life and has the distinction of permanent continuity. Today Skeezix is married and has children, and Uncle Walt and Auntie Blossom (who Walt married a few years after Skeezix's arrival) are enjoying their grandchildren.

The main character, Uncle Walt, was depicted in one of the comic strip character toys in the 1932 series made by Tootsietoy. He is driving a red roadster — how fitting for him and "Gasoline Alley"! Frank King, its author, after two years at the Chicago Art Academy and three different newspapers, ended up at the *Chicago Tribune* where "Gasoline Alley" was conceived in 1919. The strip caught the public's fancy and is carried on today by Dick and Perry Moores.

Uncle Walt in a Roadster, by Tootsietoy

68

SMITTY

Smitty, the young office boy created by Walter Berndt, has held the interest of comic strip readers for over fifty years. When Smitty first made his appearance in 1922, he immediately captured an audience of millions of Americans. His determination to hit the big time seemed to be the mood of America in the pre-depression era. The give-and-take between Smitty and his boss, Mr. Bailey, is reminiscent of the whole "first step on the ladder" tradition.

The Smitty Scooter, manufactured by the Marx Toy Company around 1930, is orange with black stripes and has a red handle and wheels. Smitty's dress is just as it was in the early years of the strip, with an oversized hat, black bow tie, ankle high shoes, and short black pants. Both Smitty's shirt and hair are the same orange color as the scooter. The action of the toy is quite simple. There is a rod connecting the front wheel to one of the gears. As the toy operates, the rod activates the front wheel. The slow rotation of the front wheel allows the toy to go in different directions. It is powered by a small barrel spring. The figure is removable, as an attachment on his foot fits into a slot in the scooter. The dimensions are 5" long by 8" high.

Smitty and his brother Herby were produced in 1932 by the Tootsietoy Company, another one of its series of comic strip toys. Smitty is driving a motorcycle, and Herby is riding in the side car.

Today, Smitty has matured to the ripe old age of about 21 and is married. However, he still sports his bow tie, a trademark for over fifty years.

Smitty on a Scooter

Smitty and Herby in a Motorcycle

HAROLD LLOYD

Harold Lloyd, whose trademark is a pair of lensless hornrimmed glasses, became one of Hollywood's wealthiest and most famous silent movie stars. Harold began his theatrical career as a boy in Omaha, Nebraska. In 1913, he started at Universal Studios as a three dollar a day extra. By 1928, he was living in a mansion that sported a private nine hole golf course, canoe course, barbecue pavilion, waterfall, forest paths, and much more.

Lloyd inspired several toys by the mid 1920s. None of the toys are copyrighted, but little doubt remains in anyone's mind who the toys look like. The most familiar to toy collectors is the Marx, lithographed tin, wind-up, walking Harold Lloyd. The 11″ toy would waddle along, while part of his face goes up and down, causing him to frown and to smile.

Another toy which employs the same type of facial action is the German Harold Lloyd bell toy. It is over 6″ high and operates by squeezing it in your hand.

Harold Lloyd was also made in a small, wind-up celluloid figure, which vibrates when wound.

Harold Lloyd, by Marx

Celluloid, wind-up Harold Lloyd

Harold Lloyd bell toy (German)

MOON MULLINS

The pursuit of the beautiful dame and an easy buck, plus the everpresent precociousness of the young cynic Kayo, have been the themes that kept "Moon Mullins" in the funny papers since 1923. Frank Willard, its creator, has been described as an "inspired clown" and a lowbrow comic, always putting his actors into high jinks comedy.

The pretensions of Lord Plushbottom make him the butt of many a joke. His wife, Emma, not taken in by his self-deception, sees herself as high class, thus marking herself for the ultimate in slapstick jabs. The rest of the household includes Mamie, the only person in the original strip who worked, and Uncle Willie, who "works" at avoiding Mamie's vindictiveness. Kayo is our only link with reality; he will not be taken in by any of this. Perhaps sleeping in a drawer has made him this way, but he has no sympathy for anyone. Sporting a derby, as does Moon, he watches life, often perched atop a bookcase that sets him apart and gives him proper perspective. Moonshine Mullins (his full name) is in and out of poolrooms and fistfights, all of which seem to be justifiable. Moon and his friends are the biggest bunch of con artists to ever hit the comic strips.

In the early 1930s, the Marx Company presented the Moon Mullins and Kayo railroad handcar. There were two models. Both variations ran on tracks, as Moon and Kayo shared the pumping from opposite ends. The cheaper one featured Kayo on a dynamite box and was powered by a simple barrel spring, while the deluxe model ran on a clockwork spring and had a bell inside which rang while the toy was operating. The body was made of heavy gauge steel rather than the light tin used on the cheaper model. It was also sold with wheels to run on the floor. The figures on both models were flat tin and lithographed in varying colors.

Of the six 1932 Tootsietoy comic strip character toys, three were taken from "Moon Mullins." One has Uncle Willy taking Mamie for a ride in a motor boat; another is Kayo riding on the rear end of an ice truck; and the last features Moonshine Mullins on his way to jail in an open paddy wagon.

Today's Moon Mullins earns his living as the owner of a taxi and is pursuing the shapely young addition to the strip, Swivel. Moon and Kayo's derbies have disappeared, the scrawny Emma seems easier to look at, and Mamie has lost a little weight.

Moon Mullins in a Police Patrol, by Tootsietoy

Uncle Willy and Mamie in a Boat

Moon Mullins and Kayo Handcar (regular model)

Moon Mullins and Kayo Handcar (deluxe model)

Kayo Ice Truck

LITTLE ORPHAN ANNIE

Almost fifty years of danger and narrow escapes have kept Little Orphan Annie, with her dog Sandy, as a popular strip in the newspapers of America. On August 5, 1924, when forty other strips were using boys as the main character, Annie made a dramatic debut in the *New York Daily News.* She portrayed a tough little orphan with a heart of gold, who could almost always take care of herself. When events became too precarious, Daddy Warbucks, her protector, always arrived in the nick of time.

Annie appears to be a wide-eyed, tousle-headed moppet who generates much sympathy because of her orphan's status. In reality, she is an instrument through which her artist, Harold Gray, was able to expound his philosophy of honor and decency. The strip carries a message of political prophecy and old-fashioned morality. It has often brought a nostalgic desire for the good old days.

Gray traveled thousands of miles a year to keep abreast of all that was happening in the country. He was a keen observer of the American society and used his strip to convey his beliefs. In spite of Annie's popularity, the strip earned a record number of cancellations from subscribing newspapers because of its right-wing editorializing.

Annie, unlike many characters in other strips, does not age. The 5" high, early 1930s, tin wind-up, by Marx, depicts her exactly as we have known her for almost fifty years. She is lithographed in beautiful colors, showing off her bright red dress and reddish orange curls. Even her name is printed on her belt. Her creator's name, Harold Gray, is on the back of her shoes. The action of this toy is truly unique. Upon being wound, Annie begins skipping rope. Four small gears under Annie's feet allow the wire rope to pass around her. This is, undoubtedly, one of the most clever toys to be produced in the 1930s.

Sandy, Orphan Annie's startlingly intelligent dog, was also produced by Marx during the same period. There are several variations of Sandy. The most popular, among toy collectors, is the 4" high Walking Sandy which carries in its mouth a small valise with Orphan Annie's name on it. Sandy is lithographed in orange and black and carries his name on his collar.

Orphan Annie's Dog Sandy

Orphan Annie Skipping Rope

SNOWFLAKES AND SWIPES

"Snowflakes and Swipes" was a short-lived strip about the adventures of a small black boy and his dog. Swipes, the dog, was always getting into fights. Snowflakes often had to use drastic measures to contain Swipes, as is depicted by the toy. Their creator, Oscar Hitt, also created Hi-Way Henry.

The toy, marketed in 1929, measures 7½" long and is made of lithographed tin. As it is pulled along, the figures appear to be running.

Oscar Hitt's strip of the 1920s and 1930s about the travels of an old man and woman and their dog brought about one of the most sought after of all tin toys today. The strip and purpose of the toy can probably be best summed up by reprinting the poem which accompanied each HiWay Henry car:

Out on the highway, rain or shine
This funny bus you'll always find
Six million of these cars they say
Start out on every holiday.
With stove and clothes line all intact,
They step on it and leave the pack,
And thump and bump along the road,
Regardless of the heavy load.
And then when dusk begins to fall
Into their back seat beds they crawl,
Until the dawn of another day,
When they resume their merry way.
And so the cartoonist, Oscar Hitt
Has made this into a comic strip
That runs in papers far and wide,
For folks who read life's funny side,
And, we in turn, have made a toy,
That's sure to bring a lot of joy,
To every little girl and boy.

HI-WAY HENRY

The Hi-Way Henry car, marketed in the late 1920s, is a brilliantly lithographed, tin wind-up which measures 10″ long. This very rare comic strip character toy is next to impossible to find in a complete state. There were many parts that were either loose fitting or removable. The parts most often missing are either the stove, which came complete with stove pipe and wash tub and board, or the clothes line, which rides atop the car. Actually, the clothes line was a homemade antenna for Hi-Way Henry's wife's radio. Originally, a string ran from a tiny hole in the clothes line to another small hole in the headphones she is wearing. Both figures are flat tin and lithographed on both side. The front end of the car is actually a shingle-roofed dog house where their pet dog, Henry IV, travels. The action of the toy is a series of jerky, unpredictable moves which are highlighted by the front end raising off the floor. Many consider the Hi-Way Henry car to have been one of the first of the erratic movement toys.

JOE PALOOKA

Ham Fisher, creator of Joe Palooka, encountered, in 1927, an enormous amount of difficulty trying to get anyone to accept his new strip. Finally, by working as a salesman for the McNaught Syndicate, Fisher was able to get Joe into the newspapers.

Joe Palooka represented the old American dream of power that did not corrupt. He was the undefeatable heavyweight champion with a heart of pure gold. Joe personified the ideals of the American majority.

Strangely enough, the only two copyrighted Joe Palooka inspired toys were of Joe's friends and not of Joe himself. One was of Joe's rather obese friend, Humphrey. It is a lithographed, sheet metal toy which measures almost 9″ long. Humphrey is peddling a rather early homemade version of a mobile home. When buying the Humphrey Mobile, collectors should check to make sure the plastic smokestack is intact, as it is often missing.

The other toy, also lithographed sheet metal, was of a boy named Little Max. Max is depicted on a 7″ long homemade type box scooter. The box on the scooter is lithographed with pictures of Joe and his manager, Knobby Walsh. The toy was manufactured by Sal Metal Products of Brooklyn, New York, while the Humphrey Mobile was made by the Wyandotte Toy Company of Wyandotte, Michigan. Both were manufactured after World War II and are not too difficult to find today.

There was a small tin bank made in the 1940s called the Joe Socko Bank which was undoubtedly inspired by Fisher's Joe Palooka.

AMOS 'n' ANDY

On March 19, 1928, "Amos Jones" and "Andrew Brown" gave their first "Amos 'n' Andy" radio show. Charles Correll, who played the part of Andy, and Freeman Gosden, who played Amos, were no strangers to the world of entertainment.

Correll, nine years older than Gosden, had been working as a producer-director for a traveling production company. Gosden was just starting in the business when he first met Correll. Both worked for the same Chicago-based production company for six years.

By 1925, radio was beginning to be considered a legitimate means of entertainment, rather than a novelty. Correll and Gosden decided to give radio a try. At first, they kept their jobs with the production company and worked in radio on their time off. Radio didn't pay very well in its early days. After achieving success with a couple of programs that they produced and appeared on, they decided to resign from the production company and give radio their full attention.

In 1926, they began a nightly ten minute series called "Sam and Henry." It was a comedy based on the lives of two black men. The show ran for two years, with Correll and Gosden writing all the material and doing all the voices.

Toward the end of the second year of their contract, they conceived the idea of syndicating their show to other radio stations so it could be broadcast in many cities at the same time. Station WMAQ, owned by the *Chicago Daily News,* was interested in developing the idea of a national broadcasting system. Correll and Gosden signed a new contract with WMAQ but were forced to leave Sam and Henry with their old radio station. Consequently, a new story and characters were required. This gave birth to "Amos 'n' Andy."

Amos was simple, trusting, unsophisticated, and quite dependent on Andy. Andy, who often took credit for Amos's ideas and efforts, was lazy, domineering, and always browbeating Amos. However, Andy would allow no one else to pick on his friend. Both supposedly had come to Chicago from Atlanta to make their fortune. They owned the Fresh-Air

Amos sparkler

Andy sparkler

Taxicab Company of America which consisted of one broken-down, topless, old automobile and a half-empty, run-down office. They lived together in a South State Street rooming house. Other characters include Kingfish, Fred the Landlord, Geranium, Sapphire, Ruby, Widow Parker, and Sylvester.

Amos and Andy were so popular by 1929, they were even in the comic strips for a while. Their radio series was the most successful program ever to be broadcast. In movie houses all over the country, films were stopped and radios turned on when Amos and Andy came on the air.

Around 1950, "Amos 'n' Andy" went on television. A whole cast of black actors was required to fill the parts. The show was very popular but highly controversial. By the mid 1950s, Amos and Andy were taken off the air.

Ad for Amos 'n' Andy Walking Toys

Amos 'n' Andy walking toys

Today, Amos 'n' Andy toys are very popular among toy collectors. The most popular is the 1930, Marx, 8" long, tin, lithographed, wind-up Fresh Air Taxi. Amos, of course, is driving while Andy directs from the back seat. Their pet dog is riding in the front with Amos. Each is full-figured and attached by a thin piece of spring steel, which allows them to bounce when the car is operating with its jerky motions. The radiator had a good luck horseshoe attached to it. These parts, along with several others, are often missing from the Fresh Air Taxicabs found today. With each missing part, the value of the car decreases.

The Amos 'n' Andy walking toys are also quite popular today. These nearly 12" high, lithographed, tin wind-ups are dated 1930. There are two main variations in each character. One variation came with eyes which would go up and down as the toy walked along; the other didn't. There is also a very minor variation in color found on these toys. Some were lithographed with brown colored skin, while others had black. Oftentimes these toys are found with the arms missing or with replaced arms. In either case, the value is reduced.

Another Amos 'n' Andy toy, which has recently turned up, is a small cast-iron Fresh Air Taxicab. The age and originality of this toy is a matter of controversy among toy collectors. The fact that the toy does not fit well together, along with the roughness in its casting, make it suspect in the eyes of most toy collectors.

The most difficult of the Amos 'n' Andy toys to find today are the sparklers. These colorful, tin, lithographed, German toys measure 7" high. They operate as do all sparklers. By squeezing the plunger, a wheel, which contains flints and colored pieces of transparent celluloid, spins against a sandpaper disk. The result is beautifully colored sparks. The Amos 'n' Andy sparklers, unlike any other sparklers, have glass eyes.

Amos 'n' Andy Fresh Air Taxicab

Small, wooden, jointed Andy

A very suspicious cast-iron Fresh Air Taxicab

Plate 1

Popeye in a Rowboat
Popeye Express (both variations)
Popeye on a Motorcycle (both variations)
Popeye and Olive Oyl on the Roof
Popeye the Pilot

Plate 2

Mamma Katzenjammer Spanking Toy
Foxy Grandpa
Yellow Kid in a Goat Cart
Happy Hooligan Automobile Toy

Smitty Scooter
Happy Hooligan Walking
Buster Brown in a Cart (early variation)
Andy Gump in His 348 Car (deluxe model)

Plate 3

Powerful Katrinka (both variations)
Aunt Eppie Hogg Truck
Toonerville Trolley (all main variations)

Plate 4

Hi-Way Henry
Uncle Wiggily Car (both variations)
Jiggs Jazz Car

Mortimer Snerd Car
Amos 'n' Andy Fresh Air Taxi
Moon Mullins Police Patrol

Plate 5

Crawling Buttercup

Barney Google Racing Toy

Little King

Barney Google on Spark Plug

Buttercup and Spareribs

Rudy the Ostrich

Orphan Annie

Superman Fighting the Airplane

Plate 6

Donald Duck Handcar
Mickey Mouse Handcar
Charlie Chaplin with cast-iron feet
Charlie Chaplin, by Schuco (both variations)
Mickey Mouse Drummer

Mortimer Snerd Drummer
Dagwood Car
Smitty and Herby on a Motorcycle
Boob McNutt

Happy Hooligan Police Patrol

Captain and the Kids bell ringer

Plate 7

Plate 8

Joe Penner
Flash Gordon Rocket Ship
Moon Mullins and Kayo Handcar
Humphrey Mobile
Pinocchio

Bonzo on a Scooter
Howdy Doody Band
Donald Duck Crazy Car
Andy Gump 348, by Tootsietoy

MICKEY MOUSE

Mickey Mouse, the nucleus of the Disney empire, starred in the first animated sound cartoon, *Steamboat Willie*, in New York City in September, 1928. Walt Disney, Mickey's creator, first began working with animated films while employed with an advertising firm in Kansas City around 1920. Disney had worked off and on with his small mouse friend, originally named Mortimer, for a number of years before he turned out his finished product in 1928. By 1933, Disney had produced the first color cartoon. This remarkable achievement won him an Academy Award. By 1943, he had won eight more Academy Awards.

Since his first success in 1928, Disney has created a host of long-remembered and well-loved cartoon characters. All were used in his animated cartoons, while many were also used in comic strips. Both Mickey Mouse and Donald Duck, two of Disney's most famous cartoons, are still in the comic strips today.

Disney's cartoon characters have been the inspiration for more toys than any other cartoonist's characters. Mickey and his friends have been produced in such a wide variety of toys, many of which were made in numerous variations, that I have not attempted to list them all. However, the majority of these are pictured.

Some of the most popular Disney inspired toys are the railroad handcars and trains. In 1935, Lionel, one of the most famous of all toy train manufacturers, began marketing its tin, lithographed, wind-up Mickey Mouse Circus Train. It came complete with a cardboard tent, composition Mickey, and several other items. Mickey appeared to be shoveling coal when the train was in operation. Both the tender and engine were interchangeable with several other Lionel trains. In the 1940s, Marx produced its version of a Mickey Mouse Train. Notice the difference between Mickey's early pie-shaped eyes, as used on the Lionel train, and the later type, as used on the Marx train. Disney changed the shape of Mickey's eyes in 1939.

"Mickey Mouse" (1940)

Mickey Mouse Handcar

There were five different Disney handcars produced in 1935, four manufactured by Lionel. They measure from 7" to 9" long, are made of lithographed sheet metal, use painted, composition figures, and are key wound. They include the Mickey Mouse, Donald Duck, Peter Rabbit, and Mickey Mouse and Santa handcars. The fifth was an English Wells-Brimtoy. It is similar to the Lionel Mickey Mouse Handcar, except it is smaller.

Mickey Mouse and Santa Handcar, by Lionel

Donald Duck Handcar

Mickey Mouse Handcar, by Wells-Brimtoy (English)

Donald Duck Register Bank

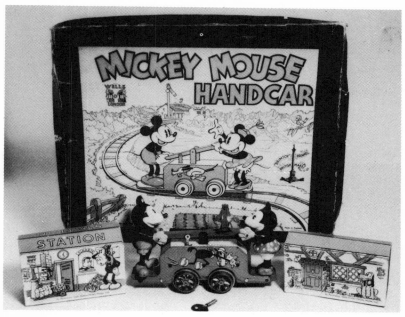

There were a number of banks taken from Disney characters. The most difficult to find today is a French, 8½" high, cast aluminum Mickey Mouse. Seven different painted pot metal banks showed Disney's characters standing by barrels. They included Bugs Bunny, Porky Pig, Donald Duck, Beaky, Elmer Fudd, Daffy Duck, and Sniffles. Porky was also made in a standing, cast-iron bank. A composition Mickey Mouse was shown standing by a treasure chest. The book banks were vinyl-covered metal. Two later banks were made to look like a clock and cash register.

Several early, French, plastic, Disney characters were made in the late 1930s. They measure 7" high and are key wound.

Mickey Mouse Treasure Chest Bank

Early, plastic Donald Duck (French)

Mickey Mouse still bank (French)

Disney Clock Bank

Disney book banks

Cast-iron Porky Pig still bank

Sniffles pot metal bank

Bugs Bunny pot metal bank

A number of wooden Mickey toys were made in the 1930s and 1940s. They ranged from jointed figures to bell ringing toys.

Celluloid was also a very popular material from which to manufacture cheap toys. Most of these toys were made in Japan from the mid 1930s up to World War II. Celluloid toys were later outlawed in the United States because they were so flammable.

Mickey Mouse on a Rocking Horse

Wooden, jointed Mickey Mouse

Wooden Mickey Mouse toys

Wooden, jointed Mickey Mouse

Celluloid Mickey Mouse

Celluloid Mickey and Donald

The most common material used to manufacture comic strip character toys, especially the Disney toys, was lithographed tin and sheet metal. Perhaps the most popular of all these toys is the early 1930s Mickey Mouse Drummer. It stands almost 7″ tall and is activated by a hand squeeze mechanism, similar to the type used on sparklers. Aided by a noise maker, Mickey actually appears to play the drum. It was manufactured by Nifty, as was an early Mickey 5½″ sparkler.

Two of Disney's animated cartoon characters, Dopey and Pinocchio, employed moving eyes. They stand over 8″ high and were made in the late 1930s by Marx.

An 8″ Pluto came in two variations. One simply ran straight forward, while the other would roll over. The ears are made of rubber and are often missing when the toys are found today.

Two other toys that used the same rubber ears are Goofy the Gardener and the Donald Duck Duet. Both employ jointed limbs on the figures.

Mickey Mouse sparkler

Donald Duck Duet

Pluto Roll Over Toy

88

Goofy Gardener

Dopey　　　　　　　　　　*Pinocchio*　　　　　　　　*Mickey Mouse Drummer*

Mickey was sold as an organ grinder in the 1930s. It was made in Germany.

An 8″ Porky Pig came in several variations, but a small Dumbo came only as pictured.

The Schuco Company made several tin and felt wind-up Disney Characters in the 1930s.

Porky Pig tin wind-up

Donald Duck, by Schuco

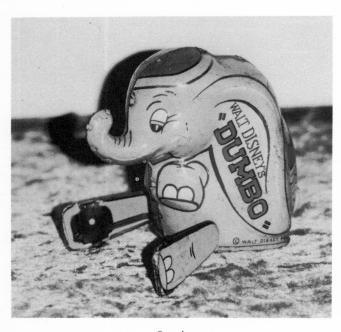

Dumbo

Porky Pig tin wind-up

In the 1930s, a clever, brightly lithographed, tin wind-up called The Toy Peddler was imported from Germany. The action of the toy caused the peddler to slowly roll his eyes back and forth and raise and lower his arm, while the monkeys swing. On the end of the string is Mickey Mouse. The toy measures 6½" high.

In the 1940s, Marx produced another variation of a very popular toy in its line. It is the Mickey Mouse Express. Mickey, in the plane which flies overhead, is missing from the toy pictured.

In the mid 1950s, Marx produced a Mickey Mouse, tin, wind-up Crazy Car that employed both Mickey and Donald as drivers. The figures are plastic.

Mickey Mouse Express

The Toy peddler

Mickey and Donald Crazy Cars

The later Disney toys which are pictured were manufactured in Japan by Mar Line in the late 1950s and early 1960s. There are a number of other Mar Line Disney inspired toys. The ones pictured, along with most other Mar Line comic strip character toys, are inexpensive and easy to find today.

Mickey Mouse Train, by Marx

Mickey Mouse Circus Train, by Lionel

93

BUCK ROGERS

In 1929, when Buck Rogers first stepped into the 25th century, science fiction came to the comic strips. Buck was originally conceived by John Dille but was drawn by Lt. Dick Calkins and written by Phil Nowlan. The strip used such unfamiliar things as rocket ships, space suits, paralysis-ray guns, and anti-gravity belts. However, the readers were also able to enjoy the reality of a down-to-earth hero, pitted against the evil forces of a villain.

Buck Rogers remained a popular strip for many years. But by the 1960s, the space age had seemed to make Buck Rogers something out of the past, rather than the future, and he was discontinued.

The Tootsietoy Company produced three different Buck Rogers pot metal rocket ships in the 1930s. All three are slightly less than 5″ long, were produced in varying colors, and ran on a string. They were called Venus Duo-Destroyer, Battlecruiser, and Flash Blast Attack Ship. Their names are embossed in the metal.

During the 1930s, the Daisy Manufacturing Company, of Plymouth, Michigan, marketed several different Buck Rogers 25th Century guns. One was a sheet metal pop gun which could be cocked by pushing the handle forward. It came in a 9½″ and 7½″ size. Both are finished in gun blue and marked Buck Rogers 25th Century. Another similar gun was called the Disintegrator. It measures 10″ and is finished in silver and bronze. After World War II, it was again manufactured for a brief time, but its name was changed to the Atomic Pistol. There was even a brightly colored red and yellow Buck Rogers Liquid Helium Water Pistol sold in the 1930s. Space helmets, gloves, goggles, holsters, and several other items were also marketed along with the guns.

During the same period, Marx introduced their Buck Rogers rocket ship. It is lithographed in bright colors and has a spark shooting device in the rear. The flint holder, which looks like a fin on the rear of the ship, is frequently missing when the rockets are found today. It measures 12″ long and came in two variations.

Buck Rogers Rocket Ships, by Tootsietoy

"Buck Rogers in the 25th Century" (1935)

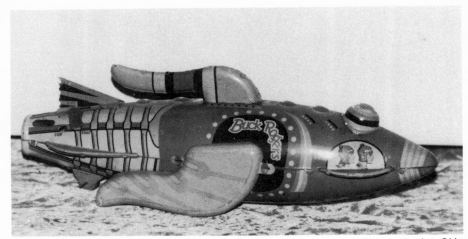

Buck Rogers Rocket Ship

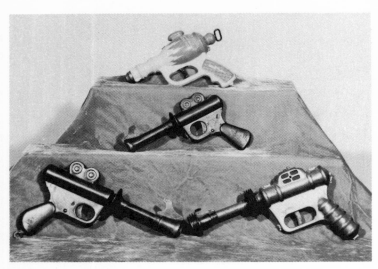

Buck Rogers pistols

Buck Rogers Rocket Police Patrol

96

Dagwood the Driver

BLONDIE

Men, all over the world, have been identifying with Dagwood Bumstead, since his marriage over forty years ago. Chic Young, creator of the strip "Blondie," is able to present his family strip in an appealing manner. Dagwood, the husband and father, suffers many personal defeats while enjoying few victories in the daily routine of life. However, he has an uncanny ability for bouncing back. His problems are simple and unambiguous. Dagwood also serves as a comic morale booster when used as a standard of comparison.

Dagwood and Blondie have been so popular that a movie series was made in the 1940s, a television series in the 1950s, and were on the radio for years. Even a famous sandwich was named after Dagwood.

Just prior to World War II, Marx introduced a "Dagwood the Driver" car. This 8″ long, wind-up, tin car is lithographed in bright colors and includes the rest of the family. This car is a good example illustrating that copyright dates are not necessarily the manufactured date. Copyright dates on this car are 1930, 1934, and 1935, which are right next to a picture of the Bumstead's new baby, Cookie. The last copyright date, 1935, would seem to indicate the approximate date of manufacture. However, Cookie was not born until 1941.

In the late 1930s, Marx marketed a Dagwood in an Airplane. It's very similar to the Popeye Airplane.

During the same period Marx also produced Blondie's Jalopy which is a variation of the Charlie McCarthy and Mortimer Snerd Private Car. Dagwood is driving while Baby Dumplings rides along.

DICK TRACY

With the advent of organized crime in America, the police could not control it and were, oftentimes, part of it. Among Americans distressed by this blatant era was Chester Gould, creator of "Dick Tracy" in 1931. Tracy, followed by a host of police imitators, has kept the true-to-life realism that makes his police story stand out, from the smallest detail of police procedure to the human concept that Tracy sometimes makes blunders.

Tracy's immediate associates seem normal enough, but the crooks and occasional visitors to the strip are somtimes frightening and bizarre. This cast includes Pruneface, Flattop, Sr. and Jr., B. O. Plenty, his wife, and their daughter, Sparkle. B. O. and his daughter were the inspiration for a toy made by Marx of B. O. holding Sparkle in one arm and a present for her in the other. It is a lithographed, tin wind-up, and, as he waddles along, his yellow hat flips up and down. B. O. is 8½" tall and was manufactured in the late 1930s and early 1940s.

Another Tracy inspired toy was the 1949 Dick Tracy, tin, lithographed Squad Car by Marx. It is 11" long and predominantly green. Tracy is at the wheel, with Pat Patton sitting in the passenger seat and Chief Brandon in the back seat. The car is key wound and equipped with a battery operated light and realistic siren.

A very similar 7½" version called the Riot Car was marketed about the same time. It came complete with a hand crank police station which ejects the spark-shooting police car through flying doors. The station itself is lithographed with figures from the strip and is 8½" long. It was also made by Marx.

Dick Tracy first brought blood and gore to the comic strips. Public reaction sometimes cancelled the strip, but, as soon as the violence was curbed, it was reinstated. Today, millions of readers still watch as Tracy fights against crime and injustice.

Dick Tracy Squad Car

B. O. Plenty

Dick Tracy Police Station

JOE PENNER

Burlesque produced many of the finest comedians to ever set foot on the stage. Some of the greats included W. C. Fields, Will Rogers, Bert Lahr, Ed Wynn, Joe E. Brown, Buster Keaton, Jimmy Durante, Eddie Cantor, and Joe Penner. Penner, the least remembered today due to his lack of movie exposure, was a national celebrity over forty years ago.

Joe Penner began his career in the early days of burlesque. One of the cigar smoking Penner's original gags was carrying a basket with a duck in it and asking, "Wanna buy a duck?" His popularity soon put him on radio.

On radio, Penner became nationally known as a top comedian, along with Jack Benny, Fred Allen, Fibber McGee and Molly, and Jack Pearl. One of Penner's lines, which was particularly popular during the depression, was, "Come to my house for a chicken dinner; you bring the chicken."

Joe Penner was so popular in the early 1930s that Marx made a toy of him. It's a lithographed tin wind-up which measures 8" high. The action is the same as several other toys made during the 1930s and 1940s. Joe would walk and his hat would go up and down. Marx also included his famous cigar, which went up and down too. In his right hand was his duck, Goo Goo. In his left hand, he was carrying a basket of ducks which was signed with his most famous phrase, "Wanna buy a duck?" and a facsimile signature, "Sincerely Joe Penner."

During the same period, Joe was also produced in cardboard. He is riding a duck which rocks back and forth. It is also signed.

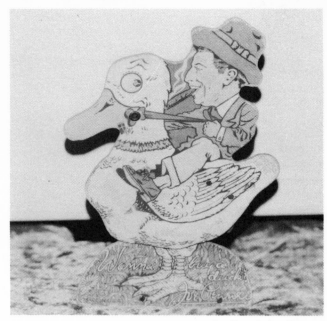

Cardboard Joe Penner

Joe Penner, by Marx

HENRY

Henry, Carl Anderson's creation, is hairless, expressionless, and speechless. He hardly sounds like a candidate for the comic strips. However, Henry quickly became loved and known internationally. Due to the absence of text in the strip, Henry encounters no language barrier, but, more than this, Henry is a rare kind of comic strip which relies entirely on the gag.

Henry first appeared in the *Saturday Evening Post* as an occasional cartoon and later made his permanent home with King Features Syndicate.

Henry's unvarying characteristics were skillfully reproduced in several pre-World War II celluloid Japanese toys. Undoubtedly the cutest is Henry and Henrietta running away. The tin suitcase Henry is carrying houses the wind-up mechanism which allows the young runaways to walk along in a comical manner. Both are hand-painted in very natural colors. The toy carries a 1934 copyright. There are several others of the same type of toy. One shows Henry riding on an elephant's trunk. Another allows Henry to become an acrobatics expert. When wound, he begins somersaulting. The last one, in which Henry politely pulls his brother, again depicts him with his hairless round head, expressionless face, and, of course, his ever-present T-shirt and shorts.

Henry as an Acrobat

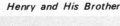

Henry and His Brother

Henry on an Elephant's Trunk

Henry and Henrietta Running Away

BONZO

While many animals were used in comic strips, only a few were the stars of their own strips. Of these, "Bonzo" was the only strip entirely about the adventures of a dog. Bonzo, who had the ability to talk, was a cute, little, spotted dog who was continuously planning some mischief. His plans always seemed to backfire, and Bonzo would get the worst of the situation he had created. His creator, G. E. Studdy, was an English cartoonist whose cartoon was carried by the Hearst papers in the 1930s.

In the early 1930s, the German toy company S. G. manufactured a lithographed tin, wind-up Bonzo on a three-wheel scooter. When wound, Bonzo moves back and forth as the scooter travels in a circle. The wheels are lithographed to give the appearance of rubber tires.

Bonzo on a Scooter

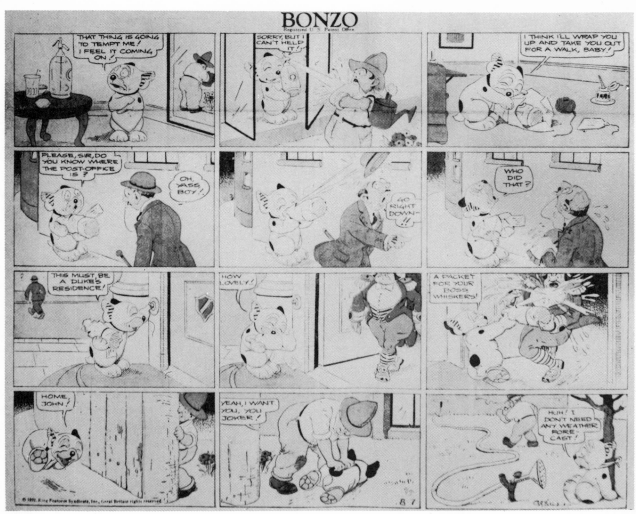

"Bonzo" up to his usual tricks (1932)

Hand-painted, tin, wind-up Little King

"THE LITTLE KING"

In the early 1930s, new strips were offered to the public every month or two. Most were untested. Consequently, many lived a short life. One, however, which was tested prior to becoming a syndicated strip was Otto Soglow's "The Little King." The *New Yorker* magazine first ran a series of Soglow's new cartoon, about the antics of probably the most-taken-advantage-of monarch ever, prior to it becoming a syndicated strip.

During the late 1930s, a hand-painted, tin wind-up was produced of Soglow's unusual looking character. The fact that almost all tin toys were lithographed by the late 1920s adds to the uniqueness of this extremely rare toy. His head and crown are made of wood. The Little King waddles slightly as he traveled in a circular direction. His arms were painted on, rather than separate pieces. The toy measures 6½" high and was not marked by the manufacturer.

There was also a 4" high, painted, wooden Little King manufactured by Marx during the 1940s. By pulling a string in his crown, he would move forward.

FLASH GORDON

When "Flash Gordon" appeared in 1934, it marked the beginning of the first worthy competitor to Buck Rogers. Flash's story was not overwhelmingly more powerful or different, but it was beautifully drawn. Alex Raymond, Flash Gordon's creator, was an expert in the field of cartooning. His excellent use of light and shadows, along with the constantly varying angle of view, helped establish Flash Gordon as one of the best drawn strips.

Raymond, before his untimely death in 1956, had created four entirely different and successful strips: Secret Agent X-9; Flash Gordon; Jungle Jim; and finally Rip Kirby. It is a distinction which is his alone.

Flash Gordon was so popular that it was made into a television show in the early 1950s. Flash was played by Buster Crabbe. I can remember as if it were yesterday when my friends and I would gather around a rather large box with a small screen every Saturday morning and watch Flash, Dale, and Dr. Zarkov fight the evil forces of Mongo. Today many local television stations are running old Flash Gordon shows. HURRAY! I hope more of America's old heroes can return to entertain new generations.

Flash Gordon was produced in three toys. The rocket, other than lithographing, is identical to one of the Buck Rogers rocket ships. The other two were both space guns. One being the Signal Pistol and the other the Radio Repeater.

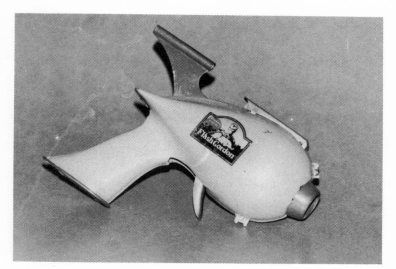

Flash Gordon Signal Pistol

Flash Gordon Rocket Fighter

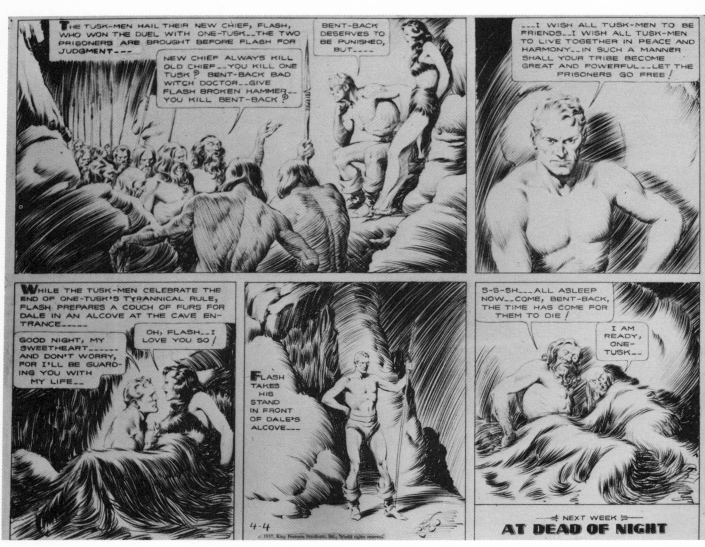

"Flash Gordon" on the Planet Mongo (1937)

LI'L ABNER

With the satirical genius of Jonathan Swift and the complexity of a Rube Goldberg alarm clock, Al Capp has been writing "Li'l Abner" for almost forty years. The strip is presented to the public on two levels: first, as the adventures of a strange bunch of country bumpkins; and second, as a satirical look at our society itself. Through Capp's pure genius, he is able to reach the American public as few other strips do. Most important of all, his humor is purposeful. Abner either exposes basic fraudulence or illuminates prejudices accepted by the public. Even his animals and places have something to say. Anyone who has ever read "Abner" is somewhat familiar with his unusual names: Kickapoo Joy Juice; Clark Bagel; Henry Cabbage Cod; Lord Cesspool; Kigmy; and his most controversial, the Shmoo.

The Shmoo was a small, friendly creature that resembled a pear turned upside down. It was totally boneless and tasted like steak when broiled and chicken when fried. The Shmoo also supplied neatly packaged Grade A dairy products. After several months Capp dropped the Shmoo, due to ever mounting public disapproval. He had created his symbol too well; it had hit the readers too close to home. The Shmoo had been seen by the public as being everything from a womb symbol to anti-labor. However, Capp was hardly finished doing complex or even controversial characters. No sooner had he dropped the Shmoo when he came back with the Kigmy. The Kigmy was a small creature who took masochistic delight in punishment. It was all scapegoats rolled into one. Capp once said he created the Kigmy so the "people wouldn't have to kick each other around." In 1957, Capp satirized another strip, "Mary Worth", renaming her "Mary Worm, America's most beloved busybody."

The Li'l Abner Band was marketed in 1945 by the Unique Art Manufacturing Company of Newark, New Jersey. Four of the characters from the strip are used on the toy. Mammy Yokum directs the Dog Patch 4 from the top of the piano while Daisy Mae plays it, Abner dances, and Pappy Yokum plays the drum. The lithographing is very interesting, with the true mood of the strip kept intact. The toy is essentially the same as several earlier Negro piano toy versions by other companies.

For over forty years, Al Capp has been parading his outlandish collection of characters in the funny papers, and America has had the rare opportunity to look at itself through the eyes of a satirical genius.

L'il Abner Band

Mortimer Snerd and Charlie McCarthy Drummers

MORTIMER and CHARLIE

Edgar Bergen, the most popular of all ventriloquists, has remained at the top of his field for forty years. Bergen and his two dummies, Charlie McCarthy and Mortimer Snerd, had their own radio and television programs. They also made personal appearances, played in the movies, and were drawn for comic books and strips.

The strip, which was started in the 1930s, depicted Charlie and Mortimer as regular cartoon characters, rather than wooden dummies. It was entitled "Mortimer and Charlie" and was drawn by Ben Batsford. Mortimer was a country boy, while Charlie was an overdressed city dude. Charlie was always the perfect gentleman who invariably took advantage of his friend, Mortimer.

Around 1939, Marx manufactured several Charlie McCarthy and Mortimer Snerd lithographed tin, wind-up toys. One of the most common is an 8″ tall, standing Charlie McCarthy. His mouth goes up and down as he waddles from side to side. Another similar Bergen inspired toy, which is also quite common, is an 8″ Mortimer Snerd, who waddles along while his hat goes up and down.

Standing Charlie McCarthy

108

Two not-so-common toys were the Charlie Mc-Carthy and Mortimer Snerd drummers. The two were identical except for lithographing and their heads. They measure over 8″ tall and 9″ long. When wound, they rapidly walk along, pushing the drum as they beat it.

For the Charlie and Mortimer Crazy Cars Marx simply changed the lithographing and heads on its Uncle Wiggily Crazy Car, already in production. The action of the cars is the same as the Uncle Wiggily car.

Another of the Marx cars is called the Charlie McCarthy and Mortimer Snerd Private Car. It measures over 15″ and employs a spring-type bumper which would allow the car to bounce off of an object and proceed in another direction. The principle behind the bumper system is quite similar to what full size car manufacturers are using today.

Charlie McCarthy and Mortimer Snerd Private Car

Charlie McCarthy Crazy Car

Mortimer Snerd Crazy Car

"Mortimer and Charlie" (1939)

THE LONE RANGER

"A fiery horse with the speed of light, a cloud of dust and a hearty hi-ho Silver" were the words that greeted millions of listeners, readers, and viewers during a span from the heyday of radio in the 1930s to the early days of television in the 1950s. The Lone Ranger, champion of justice, and Tonto, his faithful Indian companion, rode the western plains of America for many years, trying to bring law and order to the untamed frontier. As the thundering of hoof beats came from out of the past, the masked rider took us to those thrilling days of yesteryear.

Around 1938, Marx marketed The Lone Ranger Riding Silver. It is an 8″ high, lithographed, tin wind-up which vibrates as if Silver were actually rearing up. The Lone Ranger spins his lariat at the same time. This is essentially the same toy which was later put on a rocker and used with several other names.

111

SUPERMAN

Faster than a speeding bullet!
More powerful than a locomotive!
Able to leap tall buildings at a single bound!
Look! Up in the sky!
It's a bird!
It's a plane!
IT'S SUPERMAN!

Superman, a 1933 creation of Jerry Siegel and Joe Shuster, both of whom were 17 years old at the time, made his public debut in the first *Action Comics* in June, 1938. His instant popularity earned him his own *Superman Comics* by 1939. In 1940, Superman was thrilling radio listeners all over the country. A year later, Superman had hit the silver screen and become a leading comic strip in over 200 newspapers. By the early 1950s, Superman was on TV.

It's hard to explain how a character so vastly different than all the other standard types could become such an instant success. Perhaps living through a long depression made even a character as outlandish as Superman a truly needed superhero. If it was this type the American public was looking for, they were in for a real treat. Superman was the beginning of a trend toward heroes, each seemingly more outlandish than the last.

Superman, the last survivor from the far off planet Krypton, is endowed with almost unlimited powers. His powers have increased, over the years, however. In the beginning, he didn't have x-ray eyes and could not fly, although he could make incredible leaps. His power has not been the only thing that has changed over the years. There have been numerous name changes and differing explanations. Lois Lane and Clark Kent, Superman's alias, were married in the early 1950s. However, this was only in the strip and not in the comics or on TV. The whole marriage was later explained away as a dream. Perhaps the confusion of the conflicting interpretations and changes only adds to the excitement of the character.

Incredibly, Superman was only produced in one vintage toy, the 1940 Marx Superman Fighting the Airplane. This 6" long, lithographed tin wind-up is clever. Superman, who is attached to the rear of the plane by a heavy wire, appears to turn the plane, and the sinister-looking character in it, over and over. Occasionally the plane is encountered with the Superman figure missing. There were also two Line Mar Japanese Superman tank variations made in the 1960s.

Superman was one of my favorite TV stars as a young boy. However, even in the days when I followed the adventures of Superman, I could never help but wonder how such an unimaginative disguise as a pair of glasses, suit, and hat could hide the identity of Superman!

HOPALONG CASSIDY

Hopalong Cassidy, played by William Boyd, was a western movie idol of millions during the 1940s and 1950s. Hoppy, a silver-haired cowboy who always dressed in black, personified law, order, honor, and frontier bravery. Boyd, who began his Hollywood career in 1919, starred as Hopalong Cassidy in 54 feature films by the early 1950s. Then he turned to a new half-hour TV program. Hoppy, in his heyday, was pictured on T-shirts, ten-gallon hats, guns, pencils, noise makers, comic books, and even in the comic strips.

Around 1950, Marx began producing a Hopalong Cassidy rocking horse toy. Marx also produced several similar variations using other names. The rocking action of the toy causes Hoppy to spin his lariat. The toy itself is 11″ long and is lithographed in bright colors with Hoppy, in his black outfit, riding his white horse, Topper.

HOWDY DOODY

Anyone who was young enough to watch children's television programs in the early 1950s will remember "Howdy Doody." Howdy, a puppet whose closest friend was Buffalo Bob, was probably the most successful children's program of the 1950s. Buffalo Bob Smith, a great children's entertainer and creator of Howdy Doody, narrated the show. Howdy, Bob, Clarabell the clown, Flub-a-dub the seal, and other characters would go through a series of comic episodes as the children, in the peanut gallery and at home, were glued to the new medium of entertainment, television.

During the early 1950s, the Unique Art Toy Company produced a Howdy Doody piano toy. It is essentially the same toy as several earlier piano toys. Bob moves from side to side as if he were playing the piano, as Howdy dances. The back side of the piano was used to advertise other toys Unique had on the market at the time.

BUYING, SELLING, AND TRADING
THROUGH THE MAIL

The ideal way to buy, sell, or trade toys is always in person. Each party is able to thoroughly inspect the toy, which eliminates any misinterpretation of description. Unfortunately, this is not always possible. Most toy collectors seldom have the opportunity to go to more than one or two toy shows a year. Therefore, almost all toy collectors do some business through the mail.

Buying toys through the mail can be rewarding or frustrating. Individual determination of the condition of a toy is as varied as political ideology. Toys often tend to be rated in a better condition than they actually are. A toy is much more apt to sell if it is listed as Excellent rather than Very Good. This does not imply that people who overrate toys are dishonest, but rather to reiterate how diversified individual opinions are. Never expect a toy to be in better condition than advertised. More often than not, the reverse is true.

If you are not willing to risk the possibility that the toy may not meet your expectations, it is a good idea to state exactly what condition the toy must be in. Be specific! Then, if the toy doesn't meet your criteria, you simply return it for your refund. Also, when doing business with someone you do not know, it is a good idea to include a note stating that you are buying the toy with the understanding that you have return privileges if you are not satisfied.

Trading through the mail can be quite simple, provided each party involved describes his toys as accurately as possible. Most collectors prefer photographs and detailed descriptions. Sometimes the best way to make a trade is over the phone, especially when more than a one-for-one exchange is involved. Don't be shy; ask questions!

Watch out for the collector who insists "the toy is beautiful and you will love it" when you ask specific questions about its condition. Most toy collectors are quite honest, but, when dealing with someone with whom you are unfamiliar, it is always wise to use some degree of caution.

When selling toys through the mail, you simply select a popular antique newspaper or a specialized magazine, such as *The Antique Toy World,* and run an ad. Be sure to list your phone number in your ad, as many toy collectors prefer to do business by phone. Always give the condition of each toy, since it may save you and other toy collectors needless phone calls and letters.

Some people who have toys to sell prefer to offer them to people who advertise under "Toys Wanted" in antique publications. Offer your toys to more than one person, especially if you are not sure of the value of your toys. Don't be misled by full page ads showing different toys that are wanted and the high prices that will be paid. The toys they advertise for are normally rare ones and are usually worth more than the advertised purchase price. Most serious collectors will pay much more than these ads offer.

WHAT'S A TOY WORTH?

Several things must be taken into consideration when trying to determine the value of a toy. First, how common or how rare is the toy? Common toys, or even toys only occasionally encountered, are normally offered for sale within a fairly narrow price range. Reading the antique newspapers and magazines is an excellent way to keep current on antique toy prices. Sending for toy lists and attending toy shows are also very helpful. Ask other toy collectors if you are still not sure. However, no one toy collector has all the answers, and it is wise to get more than one opinion.

Rare toys, or toys seldom encountered, are far more difficult to price. Rare toys normally have considerably more value than common ones. However, since these toys are so seldom offered for sale, it is very difficult to determine a current market price. Some collectors are willing to pay large sums of money for certain rare toys they need to complete their collections. The value of a rare toy is often determined by the desire of a collector to own it.

It should be pointed out that cast-iron toys are by no means the only toys that qualify as rare or expensive. Many tin comic strip toys sell for far more than a number of the iron ones. Generally speaking, however, iron comic strip toys tend to average higher in price than tin. This is not to say this couldn't change somewhat in the future.

The tremendous expense involved in reproducing an old tin lithographed toy makes it virtually impossible. Cast iron is quite the opposite. It is inexpensive and easy to make a mold and recast an iron toy. However, few reproductions come close to the quality of old cast-iron toys and most collectors can easily tell them apart. Some unscrupulous people have hurt cast-iron toy collecting by reproducing certain iron toys and attempting to sell them as old.

The second most important thing to take into consideration, when determining the value of a toy, is condition. While a certain toy in mint or new condition will bring $100, it may only bring $10 in poor condition. I have already pointed out how diversified opinions are about the condition of toys. Many collectors, however, do make exceptions for the rarer toys.

Some of the general things that effect condition are: breaks; dents; rust; missing or replaced parts; repainting or touching up; working condition; how much paint or lithograph remains; and general overall appearance. Each of these effects the value of a toy to a varying degree, depending on individual collectors. Generally speaking, repainted toys seem to be the most adversely effected. Next would be broken toys, but here the extent of the damage is all important.

Usually price guides to antique toys are worthless. They often tend to grossly underprice some toys while overpricing others. Because toys increase in value at varying rates, especially rare toys, they are hard to price. There are many other variables, such as condition, location, and manner of selling, that make pricing difficult. Seasoned collectors are well aware of the pitfalls of price guides and do not use them. Beginning collectors, unfortunately, tend to rely on them, due to their lack of experience.

However, with some patience, experience is easy to obtain. But be careful; antique toy collecting is habit forming!

TOY RARITY GUIDE

The purpose of this guide is to give collectors an idea of how often they can expect to find a particular toy and how it is generally accepted by other toy collectors. It is not an attempt to price toys! Toys that are the same rarity are often quite different in price. Experience is the only guide to pricing antique toys with any degree of accuracy.

I have listed some 200 comic strip character toys according to their rarity. The rarity rating is based primarily on the frequency with which a toy is encountered, with some weight included for desirability. One indicates the most common while twenty is the rarest. A toy listed as RARE is extremely desirable and very seldom encountered.

Rarity	Name of Toy	Rarity	Name of Toy
2	Yellow Kid cap bomb	14	Early Buster Brown in a Cart
10	Yellow Kid Goat Cart	10	Later painted Buster Brown in a Cart
RARE	Katzenjammer Donkey Cart or spanking toy (both variations)	3	Buster Brown and Tige still banks
14	Mamma Katzenjammer Bank	RARE	Shoot the Chute Bank
7	Mamma Katzenjammer in a Cart	14	Uncle Wiggily German car
RARE	Sight Seeing Auto	6	Uncle Wiggily car, by Marx
RARE	Seeing New York	3	Mutt and Jeff still bank
RARE	Captain and the Kids bell ringer	8	Mutt and Jeff metal, jointed, dressed figures
RARE	Happy Hooligan Police Patrol	14	Mutt and Jeff tin wind-up
12	Gloomy Gus in a Cart (small)	11	Maggie and Jiggs tin wind-up
15	Gloomy Gus in a Cart (large)	15	Jiggs in his Jazz Car
12	Happy Hooligan in a Cart (small)	10	Maggie and Jiggs, by Schoenhut
15	Happy Holligan in a Cart (large)	12	Tin wind-up Toonerville Trolley
18	Happy and Gus in a Cart	11	Tin wind-up Toonerville Trolley (barrel spring)
RARE	Happy Hooligan Automobile Toy	13	Tin wind-up Toonerville Trolley (railroad wheels)
10	Happy Hooligan The Nodders	15	Powerful Katrinka (with wheelbarrow)
11	Happy Hooligan Rubber Neck	15	Powerful Katrinka (without wheelbarrow)
15	Happy Hooligan Nodders (large)	20	Aunt Eppie Hogg on a Truck
8	Happy Hooligan, by Schoenhut	RARE	Cast-iron Toonerville Trolley (old original)
7	Happy Hooligan on a Ladder, by Schoenhut	8	Cast-iron Toonerville Trolley (recent model)
8	Walking Happy Hooligan, by Chein	8	Pot metal Toonerville Trolley
RARE	Alphonse and Gaston Auto	12	HO-gauge railroad Toonerville Trolley
10	Alphonse the Nodders	11	Tin, miniature Toonerville Trolley
11	Alphonse Rubber Neck	7	Mickey McGuire wooden wind-up figure
3	Foxy Grandpa still bank	12	Charlie Chaplin with cast-iron feet
16	Foxy Grandpa bell ringer	10	Charlie Chaplin Dancing
RARE	Foxy Grandpa hand-painted tin toy	9	Charlie Chaplin squeeze toy
10	Foxy Grandpa the Nodders	8	Charlie Chaplin figure (French)
11	Foxy Grandpa Rubber Neck	9	Charlie Chaplin on a Bike
RARE	Foxy Grandpa and Happy Hooligan double-headed nodder	12	Charlie Chaplin bell ringer
7	Foxy Grandpa Flip the Hat	10	Charlie Chaplin Spinning the Cane, by Schuco
12	Foxy Grandpa in a Cart (small)	14	Charlie Chaplin Boxer-Champion, by Schuco
15	Foxy Grandpa in a Cart (large)		

Rarity	Name of Toy
8	Krazy Kat on a Platform
8	Krazy Kat on a Scooter
11	Andy Gump 348 cast-iron car (first model with nickle figure)
11	Andy Gump 348 cast-iron car (second model)
13	Andy Gump 348 cast-iron car (deluxe model)
14	Andy Gump still bank
8	Andy Gump 346 car by Tootsietoy
12	Chester Gump Pony Cart
11	Boob McNutt tin wind-up (normal looking)
10	Boob McNutt tin wind-up (with large hat)
7	Boob McNutt, by Schoenhut
18	Buttercup and Spare Ribs platform toy
19	Crawling Buttercup
2	Celluloid Betty Boop
14	Barney Google and Spark Plug tin wind-up
17	Rudy the Ostrich
15	Barney Google Racing Toy
8	Barney Google and Spark Plug, by Schoenhut
20	Popeye the Sailor in a Rowboat
16	Popeye Patrol cast-iron motorcycle
14	Popeye Spinach Delivery cast-iron motorcycle
12	Popeye Express with the overhead airplane
4	Popeye Flyer
7	Popeye the Pilot (narrow blue and white body)
7	Popeye the Pilot (bright colored plane)
6	Popeye Express
2	Popeye and the Parrot Cages
7	Walking Popeye, by Chein
5	Popeye in a Barrel
7	Popeye and the Punching Bag
8	Popeye and the Overhead Punching Bag
8	Popeye The Heavy Hitter
12	Popeye Handcar
12	Popeye The Champ
7	Popeye Knockout Bank
13	Popeye sparkler (1930s)
2	Popeye sparkler, by Chein (1959)
8	Popeye on the Roof
10	Popeye and Olive Oyl on the Roof
4	Celluloid Popeye in a Horse Cart
6	Popeye on a String
8	Felix platform toy
7	Felix sparkler
5	Cast-iron Felix with nodding head
7	Felix on a scooter
9	Walking Felix
9	Uncle Walt in a Roadster, by Tootsietoy
14	Smitty Scooter
9	Smitty and Herby on a Motorcycle, by Tootsietoy

Rarity	Name of Toy
8	Moon Mullins and Kayo Handcar (deluxe model)
7	Moon Mullins and Kayo Handcar (regular model)
8	Moon Mullins Police Patrol, by Tootsietoy
7	Kayo Ice Truck, by Tootsietoy
8	Uncle Willy and Mamie Boat, by Tootsietoy
11	Orphan Annie Skipping Rope
5	Orphan Annie's Walking Dog Sandy
2	Orphan Annie's Dog Sandy (other variations)
9	Snowflakes and Swipes
RARE	Hi-Way Henry
4	Humphrey Mobile
5	Little Max
8	Tin wind-up Amos 'n' Andy Fresh Air Taxicab
8	Amos walking toy (movable eyes)
8	Andy walking toy (movable eyes)
7	Amos walking toy (non-movable eyes)
7	Andy walking toy (non-movable eyes)
9	Amos sparkler
10	Andy sparkler
5	Cast-iron Amos and Andy Fresh Air Taxicab
13	Mickey Mouse Circus Train, by Lionel
8	Mickey Mouse Train, by Marx
10	Mickey Mouse Handcar, by Lionel
12	Mickey Mouse and Santa Handcar, by Lionel
10	Donald Duck Handcar, by Lionel
10	Peter Rabbit Handcar, by Lionel
11	Mickey Mouse Handcar, by Wells-Brimtoy
10	Mickey Mouse aluminum bank (French)
3	Pot metal Disney banks (all variations)
5	Porky Pig iron bank
3	Mickey Mouse Treasure Chest Bank
2	Disney Book Banks (all variations)
2	Disney Clock Bank
2	Donald Duck Register Bank
5	French, wind-up, early plastic Disney characters (all variations)
1-4	Celluloid Disney characters
11	Mickey Mouse Drummer
8	Mickey Mouse sparkler
5	Dopey wind-up
5	Pinocchio wind-up
5	Pluto wind-up (both variations)
5	Goofy the Gardener
5	Donald Duck Duet
10	Mickey Mouse Organ Grinder
6	Porky Pig wind-up (all variations)
10	Disney characters, by Schuco
4	Donald and Mickey Crazy Cars, by Marx
7	Buck Rogers Rocket Ships (both variations)

Rarity	Name of Toy
6	Buck Rogers Rocket Ships (all 3 variations), by Tootsietoy
7	Buck Rogers Liquid Helium Pistol
5	Buck Rogers Disintegrator Pistol
5	Buck Rogers Atomic Pistol
5	Buck Rogers 25th Century Pistol (9½" size)
6	Buck Rogers 25th Century Pistol (7½" size)
7	Dagwood the Driver
10	Dagwood the Pilot
15	Blondie's Jalopy
4	Dick Tracy Police Station
3	Dick Tracy Squad Car
2	B. O. Plenty
8	Joe Penner, by Marx
2-5	Henry celluloid toys (all variations)
13	Bonzo on a Scooter
20	Hand-painted Little King tin wind-up
7	Flash Gordon Rocket Fighter
5	Flash Gordon Radio Repeater
6	Flash Gordon Signal Pistol
6	Li'l Abner Band
3	Standing Charlie McCarthy
4	Standing Mortimer Snerd
7	Charlie McCarthy Drummer
9	Mortimer Snerd Drummer
7	Charlie McCarthy Crazy Car
9	Mortimer Snerd Crazy Car
10	Charlie McCarthy and Mortimer Snerd Private Car
5	Lone Ranger tin wind-up
10	Superman Fighting the Airplane, by Marx
4	Hopalong Cassidy
7	Howdy Doody Band